The Economic Role of the State

The Economic Role of the State

Joseph E. Stiglitz et al.

Edited by Arnold Heertje

Basil Blackwell
In association with Bank Insinger de Beaufort NV

Copyright © Bank Insinger de Beaufort NV 1989

First published 1989

Basil Blackwell Ltd
108 Cowley Road, Oxford, OX4 1JF, UK

Basil Blackwell Inc.
3 Cambridge Center
Cambridge, MA 02142, USA

All rights reserved. Except for the quotation of short passages for the purposes of criticism and review, no part of this publication may be reproduced, stored in a retrieval system, or transmitted, in any form or by any means, electronic, mechanical, photocopying, recording or otherwise, without the prior permission of the publisher.

Except in the United States of America, this book is sold subject to the condition that it shall not, by way of trade or otherwise, be lent, re-sold, hired out, or otherwise circulated without the publisher's prior consent in any form of binding or cover other than that in which it is published and without a similar condition including this condition being imposed on the subsequent purchaser.

British Library Cataloguing in Publication Data

A CIP catalogue record for this book is available from the British Library.

Library of Congress Cataloging in Publication Data

Stiglitz, Joseph E.
The Economic Role of the State/Joseph E. Stiglitz et al.;
  edited by Arnold Heertje.
    p.   cm.
  ISBN 0-631-17135-5
  1. Economic policy.   I. Heertje, Arnold, 1934–   II. Title.
  HD87.S75   1989
  338.9—dc20   89-33276 CIP

Typeset in 11 on 13 pt Ehrhardt
by TecSet Ltd, Wallington, Surrey

Printed in Great Britain by Camelot Press, Southampton

Contents

Preface		vii
Introduction Arnold Heertje *University of Amsterdam*		1
Part I	On the Economic Role of the State Joseph E. Stiglitz *Stanford University*	9
Part II	Comments	
1	Mark Perlman *University of Pittsburgh*	89
2	Douglass C. North *Washington University, St. Louis*	107
3	Dieter Bös *University of Bonn*	117
4	Chris Freeman *University of Sussex, Brighton*	135
5	A. H. E. M. Wellink *Executive Director, De Nederlandsche Bank, Amsterdam*	145
6	Sir Ian MacGregor *Lazard Brothers & Co., Ltd, London*	165
7	Jean-Jacques Laffont *University of Social Sciences, Toulouse*	173

Preface

This book is the result of an initiative by Bank Insinger de Beaufort NV in Amsterdam on the occasion of the retirement of its president, Kees Willems. It is intended to, and unquestionably will, revitalize the discussion of the economic role of the State. The landmark essay by Joseph Stiglitz will, to my mind, inspire this debate constructively and vigorously for years to come, measured along the axes of both economic analysis in retrospect and actual economic developments. The comments on Stiglitz's essay reflect the plurality of argument which will help to shape the future of public economics.

Arnold Heertje
University of Amsterdam

Introduction

Arnold Heertje

It is hard to think of the sophisticated economic and social network of present-day societies without the role of the State. Individual welfare does not only spring from market transactions in the private sector, but also depends in a positive sense on goods and services like law and order, education, and the economic infrastructure provided by government. It may be that the behavior of the government with regard to production of goods, redistribution of income, and managing the economy by formal laws and informal rules is considered by citizens to be too extensive or too limited. This suggests the existence of an optimal division between private and public activity in the economy. The question may arise whether a more concrete meaning can be attached to the rather abstract and general notion of an optimum with respect to the size and character of the public sector.

In reality the extent and character of the role of the State is the outcome of a melting-pot of non-economic value judgements of the citizens at large, preferences of consumers for private and public goods, decisions of producers on allocation of resources and growth, and the views of the owners of the factors of production on a just distribution of welfare on one hand, and the network of relationships of power within the public sector on the other. Over the years experience points to overwhelming State activity followed by violent swings in the opposite direction.

To provide a deeper insight into the optimal mix of the private and public sector in the economy is a task of economic theory. The economic approach by its nature has to do with those aspects of the role of the State that are related to scarcity of natural resources, labor, and capital, and to individual and social welfare. Normative judgment on the role of the State can be and must be clearly distinguished from analytical or positive statements on the economics of the State. This fundamental distinction also helps to enlighten economic policies carried out by the State. It needs no emphasis that the existence of a possible optimum with respect to the economic activity of the State does not exclude the possibility that in view of cultural, legal, social, and other aspects of human relations the economic optimum does not coincide with an overall optimum. This makes the analysis of the economic optimum no less relevant.[1]

The theoretical background for our theme is welfare economics. In my view, we can only start from the broad and formal concept of welfare, defined as subjective satisfaction of wants, depending on the allocation of scarce resources. A case in point is the decision not to touch upon nature and to keep it as it is. There is a strong tendency, not only in popular writings but also in economic theory, to argue as if only measurable market transactions matter in real life and as if aspects of decision-making in the economy that are of a qualitative, non-measurable character are outside the sphere of economic analysis. However, the economic aspect of the decision to preserve nature in view of the welfare of future generations, as an alternative to the use of natural resources for the production of motor cars, is nothing but the allocation of scarce means. It follows that there are no economic ends, but only economic aspects of public and private decision-making. In Paretian welfare theory, the welfare of a group of individuals increases according to the Pareto-criterion if at least one individual is made better off and nobody is made worse off by a reallocation of resources. This is not a normative statement on welfare effects, but a definition of a change in social welfare. In the same vein, the concept of a Pareto-optimum plays the role of an analytical device in welfare economics and is not a normative yardstick for economic policy.[2] In other words, welfare economics is a body of economic analysis and not a set of normative rules.[3] Economists who adhere to the normative interpretation of Paretian welfare economics in all probability arrive at other conclusions and insights, with regard to the economic role of the State in a mixed economy, than those for whom Pareto's legacy is a useful scheme of analysis of welfare effects linked to economic activity in the market and public sphere of the economy, without recourse to political prescriptions. In short, even if economic theory in the coming years proves able to develop a suitable interpretation of an optimal economic role of the State, it does not follow that such a concept will have any other significance for actual economic and social policy than simply being a well-founded frame of reference.

Against this methodological background I would like to dwell for a moment on a few issues and topics which seem to be relevant, in order to structure and specify the debate on the economic role of the State and on the optimum size and character of the public sector.

For the individual the utility of a good may be rival or non-rival and excludable or non-excludable. The benefits of pure public goods are both non-rival and non-excludable and those of pure private goods are both rival and excludable. There are cases in between, of which the category of club goods is an important subset both in theory and practice.[4] Recreation areas and toll roads are examples of club goods, the benefits of which are excludable and partially non-rival. While pure public goods for technical reasons can only be supplied by the government, club and private goods offer the possibility of a choice between provision by the government and the market sector of the economy. It is here that the cost-benefit analysis of a comparison between private and public provision comes to the fore. Costs and benefits may be looked at in the restricted sense of allocative efficiency, but a broader framework also takes the effects on equity into consideration. The existence of a trade-off between efficiency and equity or between growth and equity may give rise to different optima, depending on the specification of the distribution of income from which one starts the analysis.[5]

The present analysis is sensitive to the question whether one considers the State as a voluntary association of citizens of free will, or as a compulsory organization, having, for example, the power to tax. As a voluntary association the State reflects, in particular, the views, opinions, and preferences of the living generation with their rather restricted time horizon. Considered as a compulsory organization, the State has the power to incorporate the interests of future generations into economic and social policy, even if their interests are not incorporated in the preferences of the living generation.[6] In view of the shaping of environmental policy on a world-wide scale the distinction seems to be of particular relevance.[7] However, Schelling (1984, p. 84) has called the dichotomy of voluntarism and coercion false, as "so many techniques, instruments, and philosophies exist beyond or in addition to these two rather pure forms that they may be a poor way of posing a choice."

Looking at the economy without allowing for technical change has a major impact on the outcome of the optimality discussion. At first sight, the role of the State seems to be far less fundamental if there is no change in methods of production, products, and therefore wants, in comparison with a dynamic economy, which is in a state of permanent "creative destruction" à la Schumpeter.[8] One can hardly avoid the impression that in view of technical change, the optimal mix of private and public activity in the economy differs both quantitatively and qualitatively from the static optimum. This idea is the mirror image of the reasoning applied to the market sector. Without technical change the imitation of the market sector by means of a centrally planned economy is rather easy to carry out. The role of the market economy with technical change is completely different, as nervous entrepreneurs are constantly chasing each other in order to discover new beneficial methods of production, new products, and new wants.[9] The market mechanism as a mechanism of discovery cannot be imitated by a central government. As technical change, in general, produces goods and bads, the economic role of the State is not independent of the attention paid in the argument to technology. Here, again, environmental problems come to mind, which are often both the product of technical change and which need technical change for their solution.[10]

It is standard procedure in economic theory to study the economic system, taking the legal system as given. In recent decades the new field of the economics of law has been developed, in which the interactions between the economic and legal systems are studied, so that the legal system is no longer considered to be given. Under the influence of the work by Coase (1988), in particular, prevailing laws are approached as the result of a choice made from a set of potential laws. The choice also depends on allocative and distributive considerations of an economic nature. In my view, Coase is right in arguing that it is a necessity to incorporate transaction costs into the analysis, since so much that happens in the economic system is designed either to reduce transaction costs or to make possible what their existence prevents.[11] The debate on the optimal economic role of the State also involves a discussion of alternative social institutions, with divergent levels of transaction costs. It follows that, without the economic analysis of law being incorporated into our reasoning, the outcome of our discussion will be far less relevant. Just to give an example: the existence and development of the underground economy can be better understood with the help of the assumption that citizens consider laws and rules as a starting-point for their economic and social behavior. In trying to maximize individual welfare, they estimate the costs and benefits of violating the law. Laws may, therefore, differ in how effectively they meet the policy requirements of the government.

The principle of reciprocity with respect to external effects, as made explicit by the Coase Theorem, stems directly from the idea of studying the economic and legal systems simultaneously. While according to the traditional Pigovian scheme it is the polluter who has to pay, in the Coasian set-up both parties cause the damage as a joint product of their allocation of resources, which throws a completely new light on the significance of legal measures for restoring welfare.

The optimal mix of private and public activity also depends on the question whether one restricts the possible role of the State to allocation and distribution, or also takes stabilization policy into consideration. Stabilization policy takes into account not only demand management of the economy, but also, in principle, elements of supply management (Bruno and Sachs, 1985, p. 275). Leaving aside theories of macroeconomic equilibrium and disequilibrium narrows the scope of economic policy. "The modern disequilibrium paradigm considers that policy interventions are needed to compensate for market failures and price rigidities" (Hénin, 1986). A disequilibrium approach to unemployment almost certainly shifts the attention in the policy sphere from non- or modest intervention to more intervention by the government, even more so if not only efficiency but also distribution is taken into account (Allais, 1977, pp. 241–2).

The State may be considered as an institution, based on the voluntary association of its citizens, or as being compulsory in nature. Citizens may be assumed to measure welfare by the yardstick of money (not being confronted by technical change and environmental issues), to be interested only in basic public goods like defense, to behave according to the given laws of the State, not to expect a government employment policy, and to attach normative significance to Pareto-optimality. But one can also start from the assumption that welfare in the formal and subjective senses implies the citizens' concern for the welfare effects of technical change and environmental issues. This concern is reflected in their behavior and preference for a broad range of pure and non-pure public goods. Citizens therefore place themselves at the point of interaction between laws, allocation and distribution against the background of transaction costs, and

Paretian welfare theory. These observations reflect differences in approach and economic analysis which lead to different interpretations of the economic role of government, both in size and in character. The vision of the economic process one has in mind, and puts into the language of a theoretical model, to a large extent influences the specification of a possible optimum in terms of size and quality of the public sector. Economic theory must expose these relationships, making sure that no ideological elements disturb the picture. A better service to politicians and statesmen, who are supposed to fight a daily and endless struggle for optimality, is hardly thinkable.

NOTES

1 Not long ago, T. Negishi (1975) pointed out that the lack of positive theory to explain how the equilibrium level of public expenditure is determined is perhaps due to "the naive belief among economists that a rational government will always spend the socially optimal amount" (p. 179).
2 I know of no scholar who has made this more clear than Professor Dr. P. Hennipman, my teacher at the University of Amsterdam. See, for example, Hennipman (1976, 1982, 1984a, 1984b, 1988).
3 For the still very popular normative interpretation, compare Cornes and Sandler (1986, pp. 12–18) and Starrett (1988, pp. 1–11) A thorough discussion of these issues is presented in Sen (1987).
4 See, for the theory of public and club goods, Oakland (1987), Cornes and Sandler (1986), and Starrett (1988).
5 A classic on this topic is Okun (1975); see also Arrow (1979).
6 Attention is growing for the economics of future generations. See, for example, B. Schönfelder (1988) and S. Rao Aiyagari (1989).
7 Compare, for example, Baumol and Oates (1988).
8 A vast literature on technical change is now available. See, for example, Dosi (1988) and Amendola and Gaffard (1988).
9 Important contributions to the Austrian idea of the market mechanism – as a mechanism of discovery of technical knowledge to be applied to new methods of production and products – have been made by Kirzner (1985).

10 Let me refer here to the rather neglected work done by Georgescu-Roegen (1967, 1971, 1976), who illustrated that thermodynamics and, in particular, the Entropy Law "is the basis of the economy of life at all levels," an insight from which important conclusions for the solution of the energy and pollution problems are drawn.

11 In his recent book, just quoted, Coase comments on his path-breaking articles (dating back to 1937) on the nature of the firm and those (dating back to 1960) on the problem of social costs. He tries to explain why economic theory, in fact, neglected his major contribution.

REFERENCES

Allais, M. (1977), *L'impôt sur le capital* (Paris: Hermann).

Amendola, M. and I. Gaffard (1988), *The Innovative Choice* (Oxford: Basil Blackwell).

Arrow, K. J. (1979), "The trade-off between growth and equity," *Theory for Economic Efficiency, Essays in Honor of A. P. Lerner* (Cambridge, MA: MIT Press), pp. 1–11.

Baumol, W. J. and W. E. Oates (1988), *The Theory of Environmental Policy*, 2nd edition, (Cambridge: Cambridge University Press).

Bruno, M. and J. Sachs (1985), *The Economics of Worldwide Stagflation*, (Oxford: Basil Blackwell).

Coase, R. (1988), *The Firm, the Market, and the Law* (Chicago: University of Chicago Press, 1988).

Cornes, R. and T. Sandler (1986), *The Theory of Externalities, Public Goods, and Club Goods*, (Cambridge: Cambridge University Press).

Dosi, G., C. Freeman, R. Nelson, G. Silverberg, and L. Soete (eds) (1988), *Technical Change and Economic Theory* (London: Pinter).

Georgescu-Roegen, N. (1967), *Analytical Economics*, (Cambridge, MA: Harvard University Press).

Georgescu-Roegen, N. (1971), *The Entropy Law and the Economic Process* (Cambridge, MA: Harvard University Press).

Georgescu-Roegen, N. (1976), *Energy and Economic Myths* (New York: Pergamon Press).

Hénin, P. Y. (1986), *Macrodynamics: Fluctuations and growth* (London: Routledge).

Hennipman, P. (1976), "Pareto optimality: Value judgement or analytical tool?," *Relevance and Precision, Essays in Honour of Pieter de Wolff* (Alphen aan den Rijn: Samson), pp. 39–69.

Hennipman, P. (1982), "Welfare economics in an impasse? Some observations on Mishan's vision," *The Economist*, pp. 457–64.

Hennipman, P. (1984a), "Normative or positive: Mishan's half-way house," *The Economist*, 86–99.

Hennipman, P. (1984b), "The nature of welfare economics: A final note," *The Economist*, p. 238.

Hennipman, P. (1988), "A new look at the ordinalist revolution: Comments on Cooter and Rappoport," *Journal of Economic Literature*, 26, pp. 80–6.

Kirzner, I. M. (1985), *Discovery and the Capitalist Process* (Chicago: University of Chicago Press).

Negishi, T. (1975), *Microeconomic Foundations of Keynesian Macroeconomics* (Amsterdam: North-Holland).

Oakland, W. H. (1987), "Theory of public goods," *Handbook of Public Economics*, vol. II (Amsterdam: North-Holland), pp. 485–535.

Okun, A. M. (1975), *Equality and Efficiency, the Big Tradeoff* (Washington, DC: Brookings Institution).

Rao Aiyagari, S. (1989), "Equilibrium: existence of an overlapping generations model with altruistic preferences," *Journal of Economic Theory*, 47, pp. 130–52.

Schelling, T. C. (1984), *Choice and Consequence* (Cambridge, MA: Harvard University Press).

Schönfelder, B. (1988), "Relevance and irrelevance of the Barro Irrelevance Theorem," *Journal of Economics*, 48, pp. 333–54.

Sen, A. (1987), *On Ethics and Economics* (Oxford: Basil Blackwell).

Starrett, D. A. (1988), *Foundations of Public Economics* (Cambridge: Cambridge University Press).

Part I

On the Economic Role of the State

Joseph E. Stiglitz

On the Economic Role of the State

*Joseph E. Stiglitz**

Background and an Overview of the Problem	12
The Distinctive Nature of Government as an Economic Organization	21
A Caveat	22
A Qualification	23
Some Important Consequences	23
Choice of Leadership	24
Fiduciary Responsibilities	26
Employment Constraints	26
Equity Constraints	28
Four Fallacies Concerning the Public and Private Sectors	30
Nationalized Industries Act in the Public Interest	31
Government is Everywhere and at All Times Inefficient	32
The Control and Planning Fallacies	33
The Coase Fallacy	36
A Generalized Coase Fallacy	36
Advantages and Disadvantages of State Economic Activity	37
Market Failures	38
Pervasiveness of Market Failures	38
Public Failures	39
Redistribution	39
Alternative Forms of Intervention	40
Public Production and the Fundamental Privatization Theorem	41
Four Advantages of the State in Correcting Market Failures	42
The Power to Tax	42
The Power to Proscribe	42
The Power to Punish	43
Transactions Costs	43
Organizational Costs	43

* This paper was prepared with financial support from the Olin Foundation, the National Science Foundation, and the Hoover Institution, all of whom are gratefully acknowledged.

Free Rider Problems	43
Informationally Imperfect Markets	43
Adverse Selection	44
Public Failures	45
Similarities between Public and Market Failures: Imperfect Information and Incomplete Markets	45
The Problem of Redistribution	46
Merit Goods	48
Binding Commitments	49
Property Rights and Incentives	50
Absence of Competition	52
Perspectives on Some Characteristics of Government	54
Red Tape	54
Powerlessness and Conservatism	55
Economic Policy	56
Monopoly	57
Competition	58
Decentralization	58
Education: An Example	59
Other Advantages of Decentralization	60
Redistribution	61
Openness in Government	62
Two Examples	64
Government Retirement Programs	64
Unemployment Insurance and the Human Capital Bank	64
Concluding Remarks	66

This paper attempts to put into a new perspective the economic role of the State, to provide insights both into the *descriptive* questions concerning its evolving role and into the *normative* questions concerning what *should* be its role.

BACKGROUND AND AN OVERVIEW OF THE PROBLEM

Though not all government activities involve questions of resource allocation, many, perhaps most, do and hence fall within the purview of this paper.¹ Some simple statistics throw some light on the growth of government:² while today, in the US, government expenditures amount to slightly more than a third of national production, in 1913, on the eve of World War I, they were less than 10 percent, and as recently as 1930 they were but 11 percent of GNP. And the share in the US is among the lowest of the major industrialized countries: public sector expenditures in France, Germany, and Italy amount to roughly half of GNP.³

But statistics on expenditures alone do not tell the whole story. Government regulation of business, though it had its origins in the US more than a century ago, did not take on the pervasive role that it plays today until the New Deal, part of the aftermath of the Great Depression. The income tax (both the individual and the corporate tax) became of central importance, both in individual and corporate decision making, only during the past half century.

There are various ways of categorizing the economic activities of government. Richard Musgrave, in his classic study *The Theory of Public Finance*, distinguished among three roles: economic stabilization (maintaining the economy at full employment), allocation, and redistribution.⁴ This paper focuses on the latter two.

Stiglitz (1988a) distinguishes between the role of government in production and in consumption, with how it affects the answers to the questions of "how goods are produced" on the one hand, and "what gets produced" and "for whom it gets produced" on the other.

Government affects private production and is directly involved in production itself. It affects private production through the legal system and regulatory mechanisms, through direct and indirect subsidies (subsidies through the tax system, sometimes called tax expenditures), through lending activity (both direct loans and loan guarantees), and through publicly provided services. In the US, direct government production is more limited than in many European countries (see figure 1), defense and education being the most important of its responsibilities. But as in almost all other advanced countries, the post office and the central bank are effectively government institutions. Government takes primary responsibility for providing transportation infrastructure, roads, airports, and harbors. And in the US, while almost all local communities take responsibility for sewage and fire protection,⁵ many of them take on the additional responsibilities of garbage collection and providing water.

Figure 1 Levels of public ownership in different industries in different countries

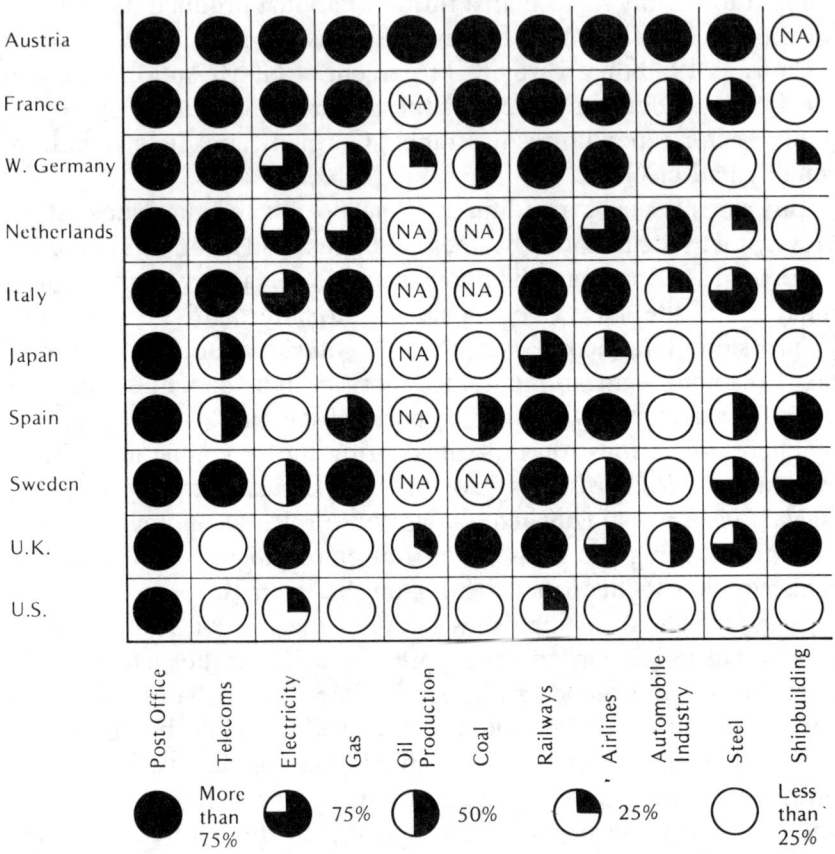

Source: *Financial Times* (10 December 1986), based on *AMEX Bank Review*.
Reprinted from J. E. Stiglitz, *Economics of the Public Sector*, 2nd edition (New York: W. W. Norton, 1988). Reprinted with permission.

We conventionally distinguish between government expenditures that redistribute income (that affect who consumes what goods) and those that represent direct purchases of goods and services. Within the latter, we distinguish between *pure public goods*, goods which are in effect collectively consumed (such as defense), and *publicly provided private goods*. The latter are goods which, in principle, could be – and frequently are – privately provided. Education and medical care are two examples of publicly provided private goods. To give some order of magnitudes, of total US government expenditures (federal and state), approximately two-thirds is for purchases, and one-third for redistribution: at the federal level, however, 60 percent of expenditures are redistributive, 40 percent purchases.[6]

Though there are links between government production and "consumption," the two are distinct. In the US, most of government production is for goods directly "consumed" by the government (provided freely to individuals) – education, defense, and police protection. But, as table 1 illustrates, government produces privately consumed goods (like rail services), and purchases publicly consumed goods (like military aircraft) from the private sector.

Table 1 THE VARIETY OF ARRANGEMENTS BY WHICH GOODS ARE PRODUCED AND PAID FOR

Who Is the Producer?	Who Pays?	
	Private Sector (80% of GNP)	Public Sector (20% of GNP)
Public Sector (12% of GNP)	Some electricity Rail	Education Police protection
Private Sector (88% of GNP)	Toothpaste Most housing	Most hospital services Garbage collection (in some communities) Air Force airplanes Army tanks

Notes: Most, but not all, goods produced in the public sector are financed by it. The government also pays for many goods produced by the private sector, especially hospital services and defense equipment. Percentages are for 1986.
Source: Survey of Current Business (July 1987), Tables 3.15 and 6.1.
 Reprinted from J. E. Stiglitz, *Economics of the Public Sector,* 2nd edition (New York: W. W. Norton, 1988). Reprinted with permission.

Thus, the question of the economic role of the government is concerned not just with the size of the government, but also with the appropriate tasks for it to undertake.

The 1980s have witnessed a reassessment of the role of the government. In country after country, officials publicly committed to the principle of a more limited role for government have been elected. Perhaps surprisingly, these attitudes have not yet been reflected strongly in the US data on expenditures. The growth in government expenditure (other than defense) has indeed been halted, but this can be traced to the mid-1970s, not to the Reagan years (see figure 2).

Figure 2 The growth of the public sector in the United States, 1929–1986

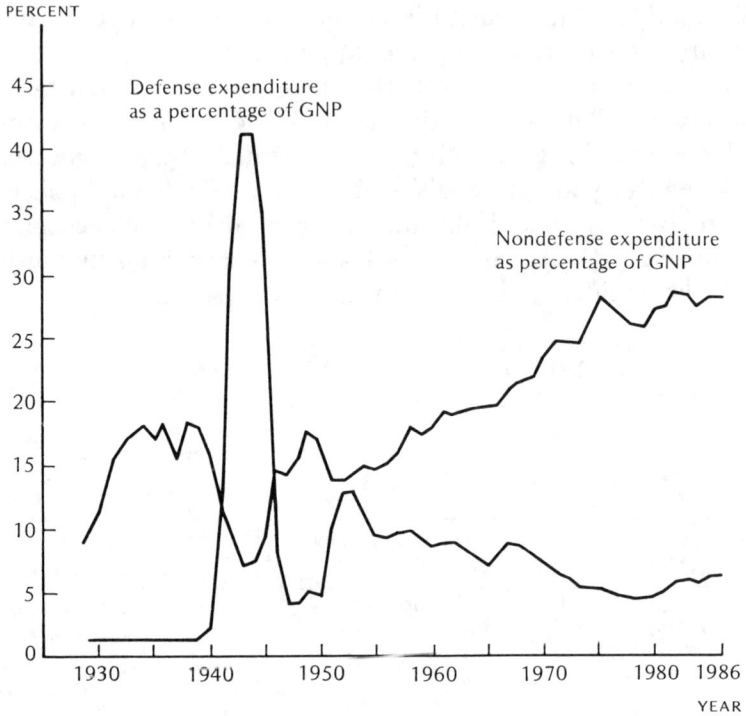

Notes: Defense expenditures as a percentage of GNP declined slowly after the Korean War, with a slight increase during the Vietnam War, and they have grown in recent years under President Reagan. By contrast, the percentage of government expenditure on non-defense items has slightly declined in recent years. Defense expenditures shown do not include veterans' benefits and military retirement.

Sources: US Department of Commerce, *National Income and Product Accounts, 1929–1982*, Tables 1.1, 3.1, 3.15; *Survey of Current Business* (July 1987), Tables 1.1, 3.1, 3.15.
  Reprinted from J. E. Stiglitz, *Economics of the Public Sector*, 2nd edition (New York: W. W. Norton, 1988). Reprinted with permission.

There has been some debate about the causes of the marked increase in government expenditures during the past 50 years revealed by the figure. Some have suggested that individuals like to consume more public goods as they get wealthier – public expenditures are like luxury goods. Western countries have experienced marked increases in income, and this has been reflected in increased expenditures on all luxury goods, including government. Though a comparison of expenditures of countries with different per capita income shows that there may be some truth in this explanation – on average, wealthier countries do spend more on government – the link is a loose one (see figure 3). There have been marked changes in mores – in attitudes towards the poor and the elderly – which undoubtedly account for much of the change. There is now a widespread perception that government has a responsibility to provide for the elderly. Figure 4 makes clear that (again for the US) much of the increased government expenditure can be attributed to increases in social insurance – in particular payments of income and provision of medical

Figure 3 Government outlays as a percentage of GNP, 1982

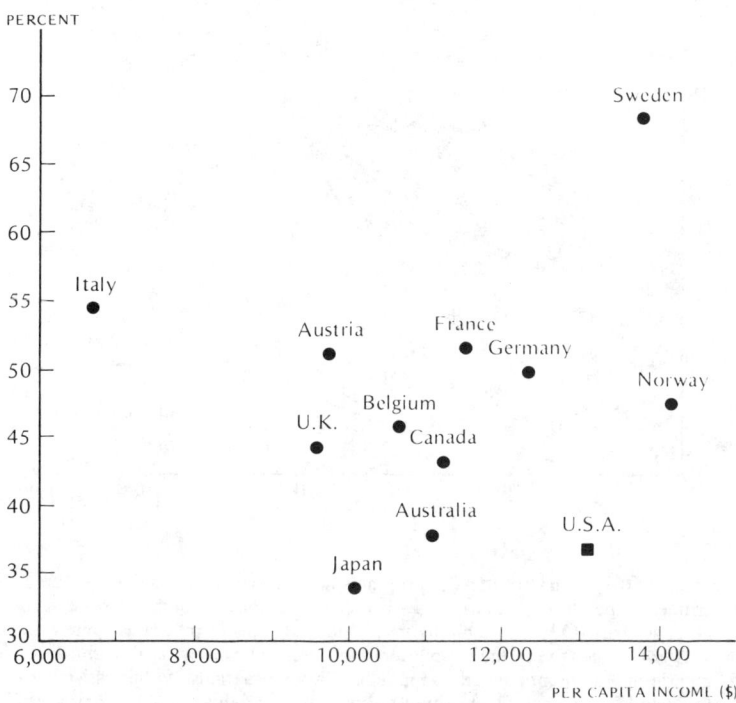

Notes: Compared to other industrial countries with similar per capita income, US government outlays rank rather low as a percentage of national income.

Sources: United Nations, *National Accounts and Statistics: Government Accounts and Tables, 1983*; United Nations Yearbook, 1986; International Monetary Fund, *International Financial Statistics, 1987*
  Reprinted from J. E. Stiglitz, *Economics of the Public Sector*, 2nd edition (New York: W. W. Norton, 1988). Reprinted with permission.

Figure 4 Government transfers and interest payments as a percentage of total government expenditures

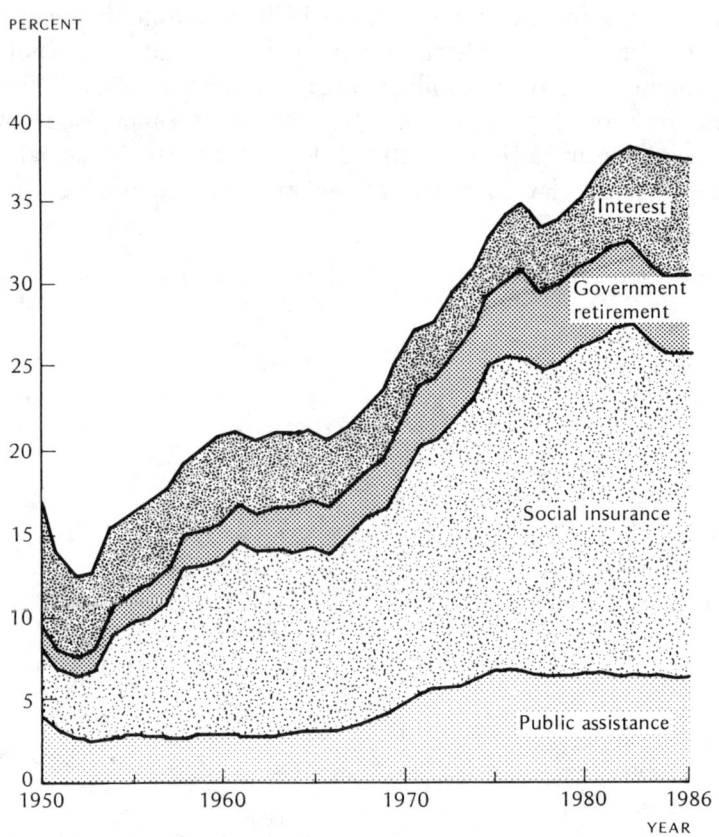

Notes: Since 1950, government transfer programs have grown from less than 10 percent of total government expenditure to more than 30 percent, with the bulk of the increase accounted for by social security (OASDI). This figure includes as transfer programs some expenditures, such as government retirement programs, that might properly be thought of as deferred compensation. It does not include some redistributive programs. (Public assistance programs do not include some items, such as housing assistance and the school lunch program.) It does show, however, the major sources of increase in transfer payments.

Source: *Survey of Current Business* (July 1987), Tables, 1.1, 3.1, 3.15.
  Reprinted from J. E. Stiglitz, *Economics of the Public Sector*, 2nd edition (New York: W. W. Norton, 1988). Reprinted with permission.

care to the elderly; the growth of public assistance, about which there has been much debate, appears to bear little of the responsibility for the growth of government expenditures.[7] Figure 5 shows that even after this marked growth in social security expenditures, they remain much lower (as a percentage of GNP) than in many European countries.

But what is at issue is not just the level of government expenditures. In Europe and Japan there has been a widespread feeling that the government should be less involved in production, and there has been

Figure 5 Public sector programs as a percentage of GNP in five countries, 1982

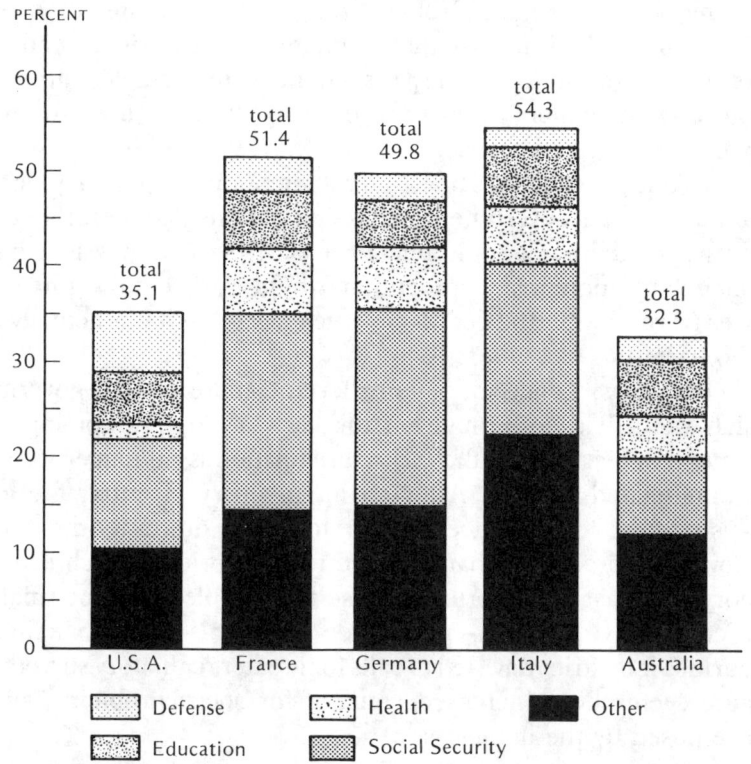

Notes: In spite of the growth of government expenditure in the United States, we see here that compared to four other industrial countries, only Australia has lower expenditures as a percentage of GNP.

Sources: United Nations, *National Accounts Statistics, Government Accounts and Tables, 1983 Yearbook*, Country Table 2.3; *Survey of Current Business* (July 1986), Table 3.14.
  Reprinted from J. E. Stiglitz, *Economics of the Public Sector*, 2nd edition (New York: W. W. Norton, 1988). Reprinted with permission.

a wave of privatizations of public enterprises. President Reagan, not to be outdone, set up a Privatization Commission, but the Commission could not come up with any good public enterprises to privatize.

Many of the industries which were being privatized in Europe and Japan were already in private hands in the US. Government exerted its influence through regulation, and in the US there was a movement to weaken the role of government in regulation. There were dramatic examples: airline, trucking, and gas deregulation. But there were equally important but less dramatic changes in policy: for instance, the standards for government intervention in anti-trust cases (including unfair trade practices) were raised.[8] George Stigler of the University of Chicago received a Nobel Prize, partly for his theories of regulation; he had argued that regulatory commissions tend to be captured by the industry they are intended to regulate; rather than protecting consumers against the industry, they are used to enforce government-created cartels.[9]

Thus one view that became, at least temporarily, quite popular held that not only was government intervention unneeded – even in industries where there was only one firm (say, because it was a natural monopoly),[10] potential competition would suffice to maintain low prices (zero profits) and economic efficiency – but it was actually likely to be harmful.

Today, views concerning a smaller and more limited government which were held so strongly in the early 1980s are coming under question, at least within the US. Deregulation is no longer viewed as an unmitigated success. After an initial flurry of entry, the airline industry has, for instance, begun to settle down to the kind of oligopolistic practices, characterized by high prices, which economic theory – at least the theories of those not completely indoctrinated in the competitive religion – predicted.[11] Scandals in the banking and securities industries have led to calls for greater regulatory surveillance. There seems even increased concern for social problems, such as those posed by the homeless.[12]

It seems appropriate, then, as we perhaps stand at the threshold of an era of increased government involvement, to take a closer look at the economic role of the government. The approach I shall take to this question is an economic one: in what does the government have a comparative advantage? To answer that question, I need to know in what ways the government is different from the other institutions of our society.

THE DISTINCTIVE NATURE OF GOVERNMENT AS AN ECONOMIC ORGANIZATION

The State is only one of many organizations in our society involved in economic activity. Our objective is to identify the underlying differences between the *State* as an economic organization and other organizations, and from those differences to make some inferences concerning the appropriate role of the State vis-à-vis these other oganizations.

I would argue that there are two distinguishing features of the State, from which most of the other differences between the State and other economic organizations follow: the State is the one organization membership of which is *universal*, and the State has powers of *compulsion* not given to other economic organizations.

Individuals choose to be members of clubs, they choose to buy stock in a corporation, they choose to work for one firm or another. Within the public sector, there is, of course, some choice: individuals can choose to live in one community or another,[13] a point to which I shall return later. But by and large, individuals do not view the country in which they live to be a matter of choice, and, having chosen to live in a particular country, they become subject to the State.

The very fact that membership is compulsory gives the State a power of compulsion which other organizations do not have. If an individual does not like the firm that employs him or the firm that provides him a particular service, he always has the right, to use Albert Hirschman's phrase,[14] to *exit*. This right of exit puts distinct limits on all voluntary organizations, that is, all organizations other than the State.[15]

More generally, all transactions between parties other than the State (other than theft and "accidents") are voluntary. From this, some strong inferences can be made: for instance, that the transaction must have made both parties better off. This is not true for transactions between the government and any individual: any individual may be worse off as a result, precisely because the transaction may not be voluntary.

There is a long tradition of looking at the State as if it were a voluntary organization where individuals get together to undertake cooperatively activities that they otherwise could not have done, or could not have done as well. Nozick (1974) has put forward the view that this principle of voluntary membership should put strict limits on the activities of the government, for instance, on the extent of redistribution: no one should be made worse off than he would be in the absence of government. Unfortunately, in the State of Anarchy which might prevail in the absence of government, the levels of welfare of all individuals might be so low that the dictum that individuals should not be worse off than they would be in the absence of government does not put much of a constraint on the State.

The view I am putting forward here is somewhat different: that the distinct role of the government comes from its properties of universal membership and compulsion. The question I am addressing is, what advantages and disadvantages do those properties give the State as an economic organization over other economic organizations?

Important examples of where the government uses its economic powers of compulsion abound. The most important of these is the power to tax: individuals do not make an individual decision about how much to contribute to the State. They do not assess the value of the services provided to them by the government, and pay a commensurate amount.

The government uses its powers to proscribe certain activities: in the US, other economic organizations cannot provide first-class mail services. It grants monopolies, e.g. franchises to providers of cable TV and patents to those who make certain inventions.

It requires individuals to participate in the social security system, and it requires employers to provide certain insurance (workmen's compensation) to their employees. In some countries, it uses its powers of compulsion more broadly than in others. One of the issues which we shall address later is the extent to which it should use these powers.

A Caveat

I should, however, be careful not to overstate the point: though the government has certain powers of compulsion, in democratic societies government relies for the most part on voluntary compliance. The government has difficulties in enforcing laws, if even a substantial minority objects, or objects sufficiently vociferously and forcefully. Individuals may go along with laws with which they do not agree, provided they believe the process by which they were arrived at had legitimation. If they believe that some interest group bought out the politicians, or that the law represents an egregious misuse of governmental powers, voluntary compliance may not be forthcoming.

In the US, the income tax relies on voluntary compliance, and there has been growing concern during the past decade that popular conceptions that the tax was unfair have led to increased tax avoidance and evasion; if these perceptions become widespread enough, it is conceivable that the system would have become unworkable.

Governments, aware of this, make an effort to persuade the citizenry of the fairness of government policies. It is this "constraint" which may account for some of the peculiar (from the economists' perspective) aspects of government economic policies: for example, agriculture policies which are not only inefficient, but the benefits of which accrue disproportionately to wealthy farmers; or trade policies which help Japanese automobile manufacturers, at the expense of the American taxpayer and the American consumer.[16]

A Qualification

Private sector contracts sometimes also involve an element of compulsion, though they are voluntarily entered into. *If* you wish to have the insurance policy cover certain risks, *then* you must comply with certain requirements. Some forms of government compulsion can be viewed as a similar form of compulsion, arising out of the State's role as an insurer. If you wish the State's protection to provide a minimal subsistence in old age, then you must, while you are working, contribute to the social security program. There is a difference: individuals have no choice about whether to participate in the social security program. Note, however, that the government could have taken on a quite different role: it could have required individuals to have a savings program for their retirement; some regulations would obviously have to be imposed to ensure that the savings were invested in an appropriate way. Many bank regulations can similarly be viewed as part of the insurance government provides depositors.

SOME IMPORTANT CONSEQUENCES

Two important consequences follow from the two distinguishing features which we have identified.

Choice of Leadership

The first concerns the choice of leadership (in democratic societies). The question of governance of voluntary organizations is a matter to be resolved among the members of the organization. If the members don't like the governance structure, they can always exit. An individual can appoint himself president of an organization for life, and attempt to persuade others to join. If what he provides them with in exchange makes them better off, they will. Indeed, organizations compete to arrive at governance structures (frameworks within which decisions get made) which provide "better decisions" – decisions which enable the organization to respond to changing circumstances quickly and effectively.

Because of the powers of compulsion and universal membership of the State, the governance structure of the State is far more important. In democratic societies, a few individuals are elected, and these elected individuals appoint others who are in decision-making positions.

Our concern here is with the consequences of this for the economic role of the State. There are two problems with this method of selecting decision makers. The first is that the electorate chooses leaders for a variety of characteristics; the ability to choose good economic managers is only one among these. Even if the president were relatively incompetent in this dimension, he still might be re-elected, given his other strengths. And given that the electorate (at least formally) only communicates a vote for Individual or Party A or B, the vote itself communicates relatively little information about the electorate's views concerning the quality of economic management.

Secondly, the electorate is, in general, not well informed, particularly on matters of economic management, nor is there any economic reason to be so. Public management (or as I sometimes put it, the Public Good) is a public good.[17] If the State enterprises are well managed, everyone benefits. Thus, *private* incentives to become informed are limited for two reasons. First, individuals are unlikely to have much effect on the outcome of the election. And secondly, even if individuals felt that they had the power to affect the outcome of an election, they would have limited private incentives to acquire the information required to make informed decisions concerning economic management and managers, simply because the gains they receive as individuals are such a small fraction of the total social gains.

In fact, whether in the private or public sector, it is often extraordinarily difficult to determine who is a good manager. Performance is always subject to alternative interpretations: a low level of profit could be interpreted as having been caused by bad management; alternatively, good management saved the firm, keeping profits from being at an even lower level, to which they would otherwise have sunk because of the adverse turn of events which could not have been anticipated.

Let us contrast how leaders are chosen in public and private organizations (such as a corporation). There are elections of the officers of the organizations.[18] These elections focus on one, and only one, issue: the competence of the individual as an economic manager, and, in particular, his ability to choose subordinates who will be effective.

There is an issue of the "public goodness" of the management of private corporations. All shareholders benefit from good economic performance by the corporation. In widely held firms, the same problems of voting that we observed in the public sector occur. Each individual believes he has little power to affect the outcome, and none has much incentive to become informed. But many, perhaps most, corporations resolve this: there are a few shareholders who have sufficient amounts invested in the corporation that they do have a significant private interest in ensuring that the firm is well managed. All benefit from their activities. Of course, they may supply too little effort at managing the managers (because of the spill-over of the benefits to others), but it is not clear how important this distortion is.[19, 20, 21]

Of course, if our argument is correct, firms with some degree of concentration of ownership[22] will fare better than those for whom that is not true. Economic organizations with concentrated ownership and voting rights will naturally evolve. The fact that minority shareholders may effectively have no voting power is not, of course, a problem: they voluntarily bought the shares, and they always have the option of leaving.[23]

The problems of choosing good public managers may even be worse than the above analysis suggests. The fact that each individual feels that his vote doesn't matter may actually have *perverse* effects on public policies. It has long been recognized that individuals are motivated by concerns other than self-interest. One of Adam Smith's great insights was that it is far better to rely on self-interest to achieve the Common Good than individuals' perceptions of the Public Good. While Smith was well aware of the harm that had been done by public leaders at least nominally in the name of National Interest, even he would have been shocked by the extremes to which this has been taken in the twentieth century. If individuals believe their vote doesn't count, they can let ideology reign over reason, with seemingly no cost to themselves or society. An individual can vote against gun control because he "believes" in the right to bear arms as a fundamental principle. He gets pleasure from standing up for his principles. And he can do this with essentially no cost either to himself or to society, since there is a negligible probability that his vote will affect the outcome. But, of course, when all individuals vote for their ideology, outcomes are affected.[24]

Fiduciary Responsibilities

The second consequence of what we have identified as the distinctive characteristics of the State as an economic organization is that, because revenues have been raised compulsorily, there exists a special fiduciary responsibility of the State. This fiduciary responsibility, in turn, imposes important constraints on the government.

Employment Constraints

The government is limited in the salaries which it can pay its employees. Without constraints, the government could use public funds for private interests, by paying individuals too high a salary. This problem, as several others about which I shall be concerned in this paper, is essentially an information problem. If the constraint were, "pay the worker no more than he is worth," or "pay him no more than his opportunity cost," and worth or opportunity cost were easily ascertainable, then there would be no problem. The difficulty is that "value" and "opportunity cost" are hard to measure. Accordingly, arbitrary salary constraints are imposed.

These salary constraints have implications for the State's ability both to hire the best personnel for particular jobs, and to provide them with adequate incentives.

Concern about the discretion available to the government to provide "rents" to their friends through employment – to violate their fiduciary responsibilities – has led to the creation of a civil service, to ensure that those who get hired (in other than top level "decision-making" positions) are hired on the basis of merit and to ensure that they cannot be dismissed for political reasons. Again, while with perfect information these constraints would not be needed (since the electorate, presumably, would deal harshly with a government that did not hire on the basis of merit and which dismissed workers capriciously), with perfect information the constraints would cause few problems. There would be little ambiguity about what was an inadequate performance. Information is, in fact, limited, and the rules of thumb that have been developed make dismissal difficult. Thus, while one set of constraints, those on salaries, has limited the positive incentives that can be provided to public employees, another set of constraints, again well motivated by the fiduciary responsibilities of the State, has limited the negative incentives, the incentives arising from the threat of being fired. These constraints thus effectively impair the government in the central aspects of personnel policy: selecting the best employees for the task to be performed and providing effective incentives.

By contrast, if the owner of a firm should happen to overpay one of his employees, the owner bears the cost. Presumably he has every incentive to pay the worker only what he has to, and no more than the employee is worth. The fact that it is a voluntary exchange means that the employer must believe that he is at least getting his money's worth from each employee.

I have, perhaps, overstated the differences between the State and some other economic organizations. Questions of fiduciary responsibilities arise also in corporations. If a manager of a division of a corporation overpays some employee, it may come out of the shareholders' pocket, not his own, just as when the manager of a government department overpays some worker, it comes not out of the manager's pocket, but out of the public purse.[25, 26]

But the checks that are imposed on private misappropriation[27] of funds seem more effective than those on public misappropriation, for several reasons. First, the organization can more easily design incentive structures (both positive incentives, relating pay to performance, and negative incentives, the threat of being fired) that ameliorate the misappropriation problem. Secondly, there is generally, somewhere in the organizational hierarchy of a corporation, an individual who has a distinct and significant private interest to see that misappropriation does not occur.

Equity Constraints

The fiduciary constraints imposed by the special position of the government not only affect government's employment policy. They also affect its expenditure policy, a central tenet of which is that public programs must be administered in an equitable way. More generally, fairness is a central criterion in evaluating the desirability of government programs.

The equity constraint gives rise to two problems. First, it is not always (or often) obvious what is fair. If individuals were all exactly identical, then the criterion of equity would be easy to implement: they should be treated exactly the same. But individuals differ, and the question is, what are appropriate differences in treatment.

Consider a typical issue in tax policy – the taxation of interest income. There is a popular view that "fairness" requires that all income, regardless of source, be taxed, and that it would be unfair to exempt interest income. But consider two individuals who have identical incomes during their working lives, but one of whom saves more than the other. If we impose a tax on interest income, the total (present discounted value) of tax payments of the individual who has saved will be higher than that on the individual who has not. This, at least to some, seems grossly unfair. Should the tax system discriminate in this way against those who are frugal? [28]

Secondly, the equity constraint often makes it difficult to adjust treatments of different individuals to their different circumstances. In fact, this problem can be viewed as a special case of the preceding one. Consider a child who has a somewhat greater mathematical ability than his peers. Is it fair for the teacher to divert attention from the other students to meet his special needs? Is it fair for the school district to expend great resources on this individual? Of course, different individuals (voters, parents) will have different attitudes about what is fair in these circumstances. These differences of views about equity make little difference when education is privately financed. Parents can choose to send their children to schools reflecting their own views of equity. But when schools are publicly run, a public decision must be made on these issues. Recent years have seen the growth of an increasing concern about the fairness of public expenditure programs, at least in the US. While earlier views of equity were focused on ensuring that the disadvantaged received improved treatment, more recently attention has been shifted to ensuring that there be no differences in treatment between the rich and the poor. Richer school districts have been prohibited from spending as much as they would like on their children.

The equity constraint requires not only that individuals and groups be fairly treated, but that it should appear that they are so treated. (This constraint can perhaps be viewed as a consequence of the necessity within democratic societies of voluntary compliance with the laws and regulations, to which we referred earlier; such voluntary compliance requires the perception that those laws and regulations are fair.) Just as we saw earlier how ensuring that the public's money be spent for public purposes imposed strong constraints on employment policy, so ensuring that the public's money be spent equitably may impose strong constraints on expenditure policy. There are a variety of regulations associated with almost all government programs that attempt to ensure this. These regulations are one of the sources of "red tape" and "bureaucracy" which have given the administration of government policies such a bad reputation.

In the previous paragraph we emphasized the importance that public programs *seem* equitable. In fact, the appearance of equity is often more important than the reality. Thus government farm programs are justified in terms of their effects on the poor, an argument of seeming equity. It is now widely recognized that most of the benefits of the farm program (at least the American farm program) accrue to large farmers, and that the farm program represents a particularly inefficient way of redistributing income. Economists can easily design Pareto improvements,[29] ways of aiding farmers that would lower consumer prices (making consumers better off) and reduce government outlays. But most of these alternatives would make it transparent who the beneficiaries of the farm program really are. And if it were transparent that the major beneficiaries were rich farmers, such a redistribution program would be viewed as inequitable, and hence unacceptable. Thus the *equity constraint* forces, as it were, an inefficient outcome. (The seeming public hyprocrisy entailed in this kind of behavior may be difficult to understand, but is prevalent in virtually all Western democracies. There is perhaps just enough uncertainty about the consequences of alternative programs to make the arguments of the special interest groups sufficiently palatable that elected representatives may not feel that they have been simply bought.)

FOUR FALLACIES CONCERNING THE PUBLIC AND PRIVATE SECTORS

Views concerning the proper role of the public and private sectors in economic activity are greatly affected by ideology, by preconceptions formed early in life, often conveyed from parent to child. These preconceptions have a powerful hold over popular attitudes, and, to the extent that they are affected at all by observations, are likely to be based on at best anecdote rather than systematic studies. Often, the preconceptions and attitudes are inconsistent. At one time, individuals may rant and rave about the inefficiency, incompetence, or unfairness of the public sector, reflected in jokes such as: Which statement is more likely to be true, "The check is in the mail," or "I'm from the government and I'm here to help you."? Yet when they see something that they believe is wrong with society, they say, "The government should do something about it!" This inconsistency is perhaps understandable: it reflects an optimism that something can be done about social ills, and a recognition that decentralized market solutions (Nash equilibria) sometimes yield results that seem unattractive. If the market solution has some inadequacy, something should be done, so the individual reasons. And I alone can't do anything. Only if we act together collectively can something be done. And government is the institution through which we act collectively.

This begs the question of why the collective action requires the special coercive powers of the government, but, needless to say, many of the perceived ills of market solutions cannot be adequately addressed by voluntary collective organizations, a point to which I shall return later.

Another example of a seeming inconsistency is that individuals complain about the role of special interest groups, and yet they try to exercise what influence they can on government policies through the special interest groups to which they belong. This too is more an apparent inconsistency than a real one. Individuals may be saying that they believe our society would be a better one were less influence exercised by special interest groups. But given that *other* special interest groups are attempting to exercise their influence, it is in my interest to attempt to get my preferences reflected in the special interest groups to which I belong.[30]

In the following subsections, we discuss four fallacies concerning the public and private sector which have held considerable sway during the past half century, and have thereby influenced policy.

Nationalized Industries Act in the Public Interest

The idea that private, profit-maximizing firms act in a way which is not consistent with the public interest, and that this discrepancy is especially important in certain central sectors – heavy industries, financial institutions, transportation – has been a central tenet in socialist ideology. A seeming (unproved) corollary is that if the government nationalized these enterprises, they would act in the public interest.

Both parts of this proposition are suspect. The central result of modern welfare economics[31] is that, provided there is sufficient competition, there is no discrepancy between public and private interests. While admittedly, for some sectors (such as railroad transportation) the hypothesis that there is sufficient competition to ensure desirable outcomes is suspect,[32] in other sectors (steel, coal, finance) competition is not only viable, but frequently strong, particularly when domestic markets are opened up to international competition.[33]

It is the second part of this proposition to which I want to call attention. There are, of course, innumerable anecdotes illustrating public enterprises not seemingly acting in the public interest. It is the public nuclear power plants in the US that most markedly fail to live up to publicly stated standards of safety. States have been accused of engaging in discrimination just as private firms have been. Unions have used the deep pocket of the public to win for themselves wage gains, to achieve salaries in excess of comparable workers in the private sector. Indeed, the discrepancy between the actions of the public enterprises and what might reasonably be thought of as "the public interest" led Papandreou to call for the "socialization" of the nationalized industries, that is, that the nationalized industries should be forced to act more in accord with national interests. Though recognizing the problem is a step in the right direction, words by themselves are unlikely to suffice.

For there are good theoretical reasons to expect a discrepancy between public and private interests in the functioning of nationalized industries. True, the private interests are a different set of private interests than those in the case when the enterprise is in the private sector. Now the private interests include the firms' workers and managers. The difficulties we noted earlier concerning the ability of the government to provide adequate incentive structures to its employees inhibit not only the efficiency of its workers, but also the ability to direct its efforts in the national interests, no matter how those are defined.

Moreover, the ambiguity of objectives provides the managers further discretion to pursue their own interests. In the private sector, there is one over-riding concern: profits. In the public sector, there may be a multiplicity of objectives – economic (such as employment) as well as non-economic (national security). Managers can always claim that the reason they are losing money is not that they are inefficient or incompetent, but that they have been pursuing other goals. And it is virtually impossible for an outsider to judge the validity of those claims.

There is a final important difference between the performance of private and public organizations: earlier, we argued for the importance of a large shareholder or shareholder group to ensure that large corporations were efficiently managed; there had to be some individuals who had sufficient private incentives to look to the good management of the enterprise. In public organizations, there may exist no corresponding individuals with the *economic* incentive to ensure that the enterprise is well managed.

The wave of privatizations during the past decade reflects a growing public awareness that nationalization is not necessarily a solution to any perceived discrepancy between public and private objectives. But this wave of privatizations is also based on another fallacy.

Government is Everywhere and at All Times Inefficient

There is a widespread belief that privately run firms are efficient, publicly run firms are of necessity incompetent. Recent reports (such as that of the Grace Commission) have strengthened that view: $400 hammers and $1000 toilet seat covers may be only the tip of an iceberg of waste and incompetency.

Again, both parts of this proposition are suspect. There are, no doubt, many instances of public inefficiency. But there are also many instances of corporate inefficiency. The difficulties of ascertaining whether a manager is a good manager (to which I have referred on several occasions) make it difficult to judge the magnitude of the market's incompetency. But there are some striking examples provided by the tax laws. The tax laws provide us with a well-defined technology, publicly available (summarized, in the US, in a mere 14 volumes). Tax lawyers and tax economists can easily ascertain whether firms have been minimizing their tax liabilities, acting in the best interests of their shareholders. At least in the US, the results are startling: simply by changing the way in which they distribute funds to their shareholders, they could have saved literally billions and billions of dollars. A multitude of other inefficiencies have been documented.[34]

On the other side, one study of the Canadian National Railroad, a public enterprise competing against a private railroad, evidenced costs that were comparable.[35] Several of the French nationalized enterprises are reputed to be as efficient as corresponding private enterprises.

A central question, to which I shall return briefly later, is: are there special circumstances which lead public enterprises to be more efficient?

For now, I note that there are indeed some reasons why, while we might expect inefficiencies in both large public and private enterprises, those in the public sector might be expected to be larger: while agency problems[36] are prevalent in both, the equity and fiduciary constraints may severely limit both the discretion of managers and the incentive structures which induce them to act efficiently; and these problems are compounded both by the immunity from competition granted to many public enterprises and by the multiplicity of objectives of the organization, which, we have seen, gives the manager more scope to pursue his own interests.

The Control and Planning Fallacies

There is a certain security that individuals attain from knowing that someone is in charge, and has matters under control. When there is an energy crisis, a response is to appoint an Energy Czar. The ongoing drug crisis has led to calls for a Drugs Czar.

Markets fail because no one is in charge (so this view holds). Decisions concerning resource allocations are made by thousands of different firms. This causes duplication and inefficiency. With such diffuse decision making, how can one plan? And without planning, how can resources be efficiently allocated?

The (what I call) control mentality likes nice organizational charts, with only one unit assigned to perform each task. The control mentality dislikes the use of fines instead of regulations: after all, how can one tell how much pollution will result, if you simply announce a fine?

The control mentality is based on two fallacies: it overestimates the powers of direct control and it underestimates the powers of indirect control.

For direct control to be effective, the controller has to have an enormous amount of information at his disposal. He must not only have the information to decide what should be done; he has to have the capacity to monitor that it in fact gets done. Those in positions of centralized control seldom have the requisite information.

There is no evidence that government forecasts in the late 1970s of the demand for energy were any better than private forecasts. Both grossly underestimated the elasticity of demand. And for internationally traded goods (or for non-traded goods using internationally traded inputs), putting all domestic production under central control hardly resolves the important informational questions: what will be the price of inputs and outputs?

Indeed, in some cases, neat organizational structures may actually decrease the information available. For one of the important advantages of having two or more organizations undertaking similar tasks is that one can use the information on relative performance, both to make judgments concerning relative competence and to design more effective incentive structures.[37]

On the other side, private firms engage in extensive planning. When US Steel built a steel mill on the southern shore of Lake Michigan in 1906, it required coordination of inputs (limestone from southern Indiana, coal and coke from southern Illinois, iron ore from Lake Superior) as well as the development of markets for its output.

There is an enormous amount of this micro-planning. (It is true, of course, that the standard competitive model does not describe well how investment decisions get made in market economies. There are not the futures markets which allow prices to serve the coordinating function that they provide in static models.[38] So long as change is not too rapid, and the units of investment not too large, then prices and price forecasts provide good bases for investment decisions, and the consequences of any errors, any overexpansion in some industry from lack of coordination, may be limited. Even without indicative planning, there is considerable information concerning other firms' plans.)

The "direct control" mentality systematically ignores the limitations on the information which is available at the time decisions get made – and the inevitable consequence of that: that decisions which appear to be wrong – from the perspective of hindsight – get made. Different decision structures (centralized versus decentralized) result in differences not only of how much and what information is collected and processed, but also of how that information is aggregated, or put together, to form a decision. In joint work with Raaj Sah (Sah and Stiglitz, 1985, 1986, 1988), I have been pursuing the consequences of human fallibility for organization design – and one can think of the economy as one large economic organization. We show the advantages of organizational forms which involve mixtures of hierarchical and polyarchical (centralized and decentralized) units – much as our mixed economy consists of many firms, each of which is, to some extent, hierarchically organized. Excessive centralization implies that when incompetent leaders are chosen (and it is inevitable that this will happen, given the imperfections of information, even ignoring the incentive issues discussed earlier) the consequences are severe; under quite general conditions, higher concentration of decision making in the selection of leaders results in *greater* variance in their quality; and with this greater variance, the losses from the incompetent leaders exceed the potential gains which result when good leaders are chosen. From this perspective, decentralization can be thought of as a form of risk-diversification. But it is more than that: for in many contexts, the additional opportunities that new projects and ideas get for independent review mean that fewer good ideas get rejected (Sah and Stiglitz, 1986). There are more independent "experiments." Society

The Coase Fallacy

While the previous discussion suggested some reasons why some (at least previously popular) views concerning why markets may not function well and government control might enhance economic efficiency are wrong, there is a fallacy on the other side to which I would like to call attention: there are some who believe that individuals can voluntarily get together to resolve any inefficiencies, without government intervention. This view is loosely attributed to Coase[39] (though he focused his attention on externalities within small groups). Consider an inefficiency, such as that associated with an atmospheric externality (smoke, air, or water pollution). Assume there is a well-defined set of property rights. To arrive at a Pareto-efficient resolution of this externality requires compensation, e.g. from those who dislike pollution to the polluters. The elimination of the pollution is a public good, and the free rider problems provide one reason that a private solution will not emerge. Moreover, different individuals will value the reduction in pollution by different amounts. In the absence of perfect information concerning who particularly dislikes pollution, the bargaining solutions which emerge entail inefficiencies, as individuals undertake actions to indicate that they are not very averse to pollution (see Farrell, 1987).

Even were we to abstract from these problems, there is a role of government: there may be transactions economies associated with having an established organization deal with a market failure, such as externalities, rather than creating a new "voluntary" organization to deal with each externality. Government can be viewed as the collective organization which has been established for that purpose.

A difficulty arises, however, from the powers of compulsion with which the government is endowed: these powers of compulsion may limit the incentives to arrive at the kinds of cooperative (presumably Pareto improving) solutions that a truly voluntary organization would seek.

A Generalized Coase Fallacy

There is a closely related fallacy which I would like to dispense with now. Coase argued that, in a particular set of market failures with which he was concerned, private solutions can do just as well as the government; no government is needed.

This view has been extended in recent years to a host of other market failures. In recent years, a closer examination of the performance of the market with imperfect information and incomplete risk markets has led to a number of results questioning the (Pareto) efficiency of the market. Proponents of the market economy have countered with the assertion that, if the information and transactions costs which underlie the market's failure are included – that is, if the government faces the same information and transactions costs that confront the private sector – then there is nothing the government can do that the private sector cannot do. The private sector is efficient, once those obviously important aspects of the economy are taken into account.

For the most part, these assertions are taken as a matter of faith by the adherents of the market school. But what has confused matters is that there are *some* instances in which the assertion is correct, that is, some examples of limited information where the government has no advantage over the private sector. The limited information means that the level of welfare attained is less than it would have been with perfect information; but the level of welfare attained by the market is no less than what would be attained were there optimal government intervention.

But in general, the assertion that the government can do no better than the market is simply false, as Greenwald and Stiglitz (1986) have recently established in a theorem of considerable generality. (The result is sometimes referred to as the *Fundamental Non-decentralizability Theorem*, since it shows that, in general, efficient market allocations cannot be attained without government intervention.) I explain below more precisely why it is that governments can do some things that markets cannot.

ADVANTAGES AND DISADVANTAGES OF STATE ECONOMIC ACTIVITY

The remarks of the previous two sections provide the background for the analysis of what kinds of economic activities are best carried on by the State. Where do compulsion and universal membership serve as an advantage, and what are the disadvantages which follow?

Market Failures

The first question can be approached by asking: when will voluntary organizations not work effectively? This is the question which has been at the core of modern welfare economics. Traditional expositions begin with the Fundamental Theorem of Welfare Economics, providing a set of conditions under which the market economy leads to a Pareto-efficient allocation of resources. Then analysis proceeds to identify important instances where markets do not work perfectly. These are called *market failures* and, at least potentially, provide scope for government activity. (I say "potentially" because we have not, at this point of the discussion, taken into account the limits on the efficiency of the State's interventions.)

Among the examples of market failures are public goods, externalities, and monopolies, in particular natural monopolies.

Although the market failures approach provides a convenient point of departure, recent literature has called its usefulness into question on two accounts.

Pervasiveness of Market Failures

Greenwald and Stiglitz (1986) have shown that whenever information is imperfect and/or markets incomplete – that is, essentially always – then the market is not *constrained* Pareto efficient. (Recall the definition of Pareto efficient: an allocation is Pareto efficient if there is no way by which some individuals can be made better off without making at least one individual worse off. The term "constrained Pareto efficiency" is used to remind us that, in making the comparison, in ascertaining whether there is some policy of the government which could constitute a Pareto improvement, the government is assumed to be subjected to the same kinds of informational and/or incomplete market constraints that face the private sector.) While traditional literature characterized market failures as exceptions to the general rule that decentralized markets lead to efficient allocation, in this new view, the presumption is reversed. It is only under exceptional circumstances that markets are efficient.

This makes the analysis of the appropriate role of government far more difficult; the issue becomes one not of identifying market failures, for these are pervasive in the economy, but of identifying *large* market failures where there is scope for welfare-enhancing government interventions. We shall note some possible examples of this below.

Public Failures

When the central theorem of economics held that markets ensured economic efficiency, then one didn't need much of a theory of government: no government, no matter how well organized, could improve upon matters. But when the central result is reversed – where markets almost never ensure economic efficiency – then there is a *potential* role for the government. But to argue that the government "should" do something, one has to have a theory of the government; one has to have an understanding of how the government behaves, what are its limitations and strengths.

Thus, as we shall comment in greater detail below, problems of incomplete markets and imperfect information are at least as pervasive in the public sector as they are in the private, raising questions about whether the government could or would remedy the problems.

Redistribution

In addition to those instances where the market fails to provide a (Pareto) efficient allocation of resources, the government may have a role, either because the resulting distribution of income is objectionable, or because there are some merit goods[40] or bads not adequately supplied by the market.

Here too our views of the role of the State have changed markedly in the past 15 years. The Second Fundamental Theorem of Welfare Economics provided a remarkable result: it argued that if the distribution of income yielded by the market was not socially acceptable, then "all" the government needed to do was to redistribute the initial endowments; having done that, the market would ensure efficient outcomes. *Any* distribution of welfare society wished could be attained in this manner. There was, in effect, a complete dichotomy between efficiency and distributive issues. Government's role was limited to the latter.

This view has been qualified in two important respects. First, we now recognize that there is not a neat separation between efficiency and distributive issues. For instance, economies in which wealth is very unequally distributed may face many serious incentive problems.

Sharecropping may be an efficient system of land tenure, given the great inequality of landholdings; but national output would be increased if workers received all of their marginal product, rather than a half or two-thirds.[41]

Secondly, the kind of lump sum redistributions envisaged in the Second Fundamental Theorem of Welfare Economics are not in general feasible.[42] Accordingly, redistributions essentially always involve some distortions; and given these distortions, it is not obvious that the kind of passive role for the government called for by the Second Welfare Theorem is desirable.

My purpose here is not to provide a detailed exposition of market failure issues,[43] but only to touch upon those aspects which are relevant for our particular theme, of understanding the changing role of the State in economic activity.

Alternative Forms of Intervention

First, we should observe that the fact that there is a market failure, even if it calls for some form of government intervention, does not necessarily call for government *production*. This is seen clearly in the case of natural monopolies. There are least five responses the government can make: it can ignore the problem; it can set up a competing government firm; it can give the government firm a monopoly; it can adopt regulations and tax provisions making competition viable; or it can regulate the private monopoly.

Or consider the problem posed by externalities. The government can attempt to deal with externalities either by taxes and subsidies (taxing the pollution, subsidizing pollution abatement); by regulation (proscribing certain activities); or within a legal framework (letting those injured sue and possibly taking actions that lower the costs of such private suits).

The arguments concerning the necessity of public provision of public goods only require government financing; that analysis does not speak at all to the question of whether a public good (like national defense) should be publicly or privately produced.

The same is true when the government, for one reason or another, decides that individuals should get certain services, e.g. medical care or education. It can pay for these services without necessarily producing them itself.

In fact, governments do purchase many goods and services from the private sector. In the US, it is estimated that the military purchases at least 25 percent of its goods and services from private producers. Medicare, medical care for the aged, is almost exclusively provided by private vendors.

In short, even after a decision is made concerning the desirability of government intervention, one must address the questions of (a) government production versus government provision using private producers; and (b) direct control (as associated with government production) versus indirect control (e.g. through regulation, or government competition).

Public Production and the Fundamental Privatization Theorem

In a recent paper, Sappington and Stiglitz (1987b) have established a theorem providing conditions under which the principal objectives of government production can be perfectly attained through private production. In particular, they show that if the government auctions off the right to produce the commodity, it can (for an appropriately designed auction) achieve the following three objectives:

> (1) Economic efficiency: ... ensur[ing] that those who have a comparative advantage in production undertake it, and that the appropriate techniques of production and levels of effort are supplied. (2) Equity: ... fulfilling ... distributional objectives. (3) Rent extraction: ... extracting as much rent (i.e. profits) from producers as possible.[44]

When the conditions of the theorem are satisfied, there is no need for government production; just as when the conditions of the Fundamental Theorem of Welfare Economics are satisfied there is no need for government intervention in private market decisions. But the conditions required by the Fundamental Privatization Theorem are substantially more stringent than those required by the Fundamental Theorem of Welfare Economics. Like the standard welfare theorems, it requires competition, the absence of asymmetries of information, and the absence of restrictions on the ability to contract. The privatization theorem requires, in addition, risk-neutral firms.

The Fundamental Privatization Theorem can be looked at in two ways. First, it emphasizes that, under some circumstances, social objectives can be attained using private production – public production does not have to be resorted to. But secondly, it emphasizes that, quite generally, private production may not be able to attain all the objectives of government policy. This does not mean that government production will either, for all the reasons that we have already noted. One needs to look carefully at the specifics of the case to make a judgment about the appropriate role of the government.

Four Advantages of the State in Correcting Market Failures

The distinguishing characteristics of the government – its universal membership and its power of compulsion – give it some distinct advantages in correcting market failures.

The Power to Tax

First, it can tax. Assume that an insurance firm recognizes that smoking increases the risks against which it has provided insurance. It cannot, however, monitor an individual's smoking. It would like to discourage smoking. It could not impose a tax on cigarettes. But the government can. The government cannot monitor how much each individual smokes (it has, in this sense, no informational advantage over the private sector) but it can monitor production. Because of economies of scale in production, there are only a limited number of production sites for most commodities, and this means that production is much easier to monitor than consumption. (The government can thus monitor sales from each production site, but it would do little good to monitor to whom the goods were sold, since it is relatively easy for individuals to resell the goods among themselves.)

The Power to Proscribe

Secondly, it can prohibit certain activities. A firm cannot proscribe other firms from entering a certain line of business, unless the government were to delegate those powers to it. Let me give an example where such a proscription might be desirable. When there are fixed costs, it is well known that the government should charge prices in excess of marginal costs. Optimal pricing, designed to raise the revenue required to finance the fixed costs, may entail very high prices on some goods (e.g. on goods for which demand is very inelastic, since the distortion caused by increasing prices on them is limited), sufficiently high prices that another firm could come in and produce the goods with an inefficient technology (not taking advantage of the more efficient technology which entails high fixed costs, which can be shared among several commodities). Restricting entry could, in principle, improve welfare. (See Atkinson and Stiglitz (1980) for a discussion of the principles of pricing; and Sappington and Stiglitz (1987a) for an analysis of the consequences of entry constraints.)

The Power to Punish

Thirdly, under current legal arrangements, there are restrictions on the kinds of admissible contracts – in particular on the kinds of punishments that can be meted out. Limited liability limits the losses which an individual can suffer; and even without limited liability, bankruptcy laws provide a further limit. Individuals cannot sell themselves into bondage. The government can and does exercise a range of punishments (say for pollution) far more severe than could be arrived at by private contractual arrangements.[45]

Transactions Costs

Finally, as we observed earlier in our discussion of the Coase fallacy, the government may have some transactions costs advantages in solving some market failures.

Organizational Costs It might not pay, for instance, to form a new, voluntary organization to deal with a particular class of market failures, but it would pay for an ongoing institution – the government – to direct its attention to the problem.

Free Rider Problems We also saw how free rider (public good) problems give rise to transactions costs, which public provision can avoid.

Informationally Imperfect Markets Finally, there are large costs associated with running markets. These costs need to be set against the benefits. The fraction of insurance premiums that are devoted to transactions costs (broadly interpreted) are huge – benefits are often less than 60 percent of premia paid.[46] The costs of running the social security system are far less.

Some of these costs are costs associated with "matching" policies with customers. Different individuals have different needs, and salesmen have an important task in trying to provide each customer with the policy which is appropriate to him. But one might question this argument: are the needs for life insurance of individuals of a particular income, with a particular set of assets, and with a particular number of dependents really so different, different enough to account for these huge expenditures? We need at least to ask the question: might everyone (or almost everyone) be better off if life insurance were provided universally and compulsorily on the basis of a simple formula?

Some of the informational problems are created by the market itself.[47] Each firm tries to differentiate its product from those produced by its rivals. Each firm tries to exploit the limited information available to its customers. (One of America's most successful insurance firms is alleged to have made much of its money by selling insurance on low probability but extremely unpleasant eventualities, such as bone cancer. Individuals were willing to pay a few cents a day for insurance against these terrible possibilities, without doing the calculations showing that they were paying multiples of the actuarially fair premium.)

Adverse Selection And some of the transactions costs arise from the adverse selection problem. Good risks do not want to subsidize bad risks. Each insurance firm wants to get as good a risk pool as it can. Thus, the insurance firms have a variety of (in general costly) methods of trying to do this. From the point of view of society as a whole, these expenditures[48] are essentially expenditures on rent redistribution. And it is easy to show that not only are they wasteful in the sense that those who gain from the rent redistribution gain less than those who lose lose, but under plausible conditions it is possible that *everyone* loses, that is, even those who are good risks end up (once the transactions costs, limitations in insurance, etc. are taken into account) worse off than if a uniform policy were provided to everyone on an actuarially fair basis (Stiglitz, 1975). The government is the only institution which is capable, however, of enforcing this equilibrium with universal membership.

PUBLIC FAILURES

The literature on market failures is far more developed than the literature on public failures. We have already noted two major sources of public failure:

1 The fiduciary relationship of the government imposes severe constraints on employment policy (both pay and tenure).
2 The fiduciary relationship also imposes severe constraints on expenditure patterns, particularly arising out of equity concerns.

I want to expand this list of public failures by identifying five further failures, four of which are, I suspect, an inherent property of state economic activity in a democratic society, the last of which is a common, but not necessary, feature of economic activity in the public sector:

3 Problems of imperfect information and incomplete markets, which are a source of market failure, are pervasive in the public sector.
4 The potential for redistribution inherent in the government's powers of compulsion may give rise not only to inequities, but also to wasteful rent-seeking activity.
5 The limitations of current governments to impose binding commitments on future governments (a limitation which can be traced both to restrictions on property rights transfers in the public sector and to democratic processes) may impose large economic costs.
6 Other limitations on property rights transfers in the public sector provide further limitations on the design of effective incentive structures.
7 And the lack of competition within the public sector further attenuates incentives. It is this last property which I see as a common, but not inevitable, property of state economic activity.

Similarities between Public and Market Failures: Imperfect Information and Incomplete Markets

Several of the sources of market failures we noted above (pp. 38ff) are, at least potentially, sources of public failure. We have already noted that, with imperfect information and incomplete markets, markets are not constrained Pareto efficient. When, for instance, workers are paid not completely on a piece-rate basis, they may have inadequate incentives to work, and actions by one firm have externalities on others, through their effects on the latter firms' workers' incentives. For instance, if some firm were to construct a ski slope or a video arcade near my firm, it may lead to reduced work incentives, greater absenteeism, etc. But these problems are, if anything, worse in the public sector, where pay is generally not tied to performance and where it is even more difficult to monitor inputs.

Prices play a key role in guiding resource allocations. The absence of a complete set of markets means that there are not the appropriate prices to guide resource allocations. But within the public sector, there are not the prices required to guide resource allocations either. (We shall come shortly to a more extensive review of public failures.)

Informational problems, broadly conceived, provide an explanation of many of the inefficiencies we perceive in government activity, not just those associated with the incentive problems and equity constraints which we have already discussed.

In the next section, we shall discuss some aspects of the redistributive role of the government. Some of the redistributions which the government might ideally undertake – lump sum redistributions from those who are capable of contributing more to the public fisc to the less fortunate – are simply not feasible. The government must base redistributions (both taxes and transfers) on easily observable characteristics – such as income – almost all of which are alterable; hence, virtually by necessity, tax and transfer schemes are distortionary.[49]

By the same token, in constructing public works whose benefits accrue more to some individuals than to others, the government would like to make those who benefit pay. But this kind of benefit taxation runs into a fundamental problem: it is difficult to ascertain who benefits, other than by observing usage. But basing taxes on usage (say of an uncrowded road or bridge) is distortionary.[50]

The Problem of Redistribution

While redistribution provides one of the major rationales for government actions, it provides also one of the major problems. Though within our society there is some voluntary redistribution – private charity amounts in the US to billions of dollars each year – it remains limited. It requires some compulsion to individuals to give up some of what they have and give it to someone else. This is why the State plays such a central role in redistribution – it is the one economic organization which has the power of compulsion to effectuate redistributions.[51]

But the fact that it has the power to redistribute does not say from or to whom it redistributes income or how those rights and obligations are acquired. The government has not infrequently used its powers of redistribution to redistribute income towards the wealthy and towards special interest groups (always clothing its arguments for doing so in some other garb). And it accomplishes this redistribution in a complex of ways; while textile producers may receive higher prices because of trade restrictions, Chrysler received a subsidy through loan guarantees.

In recent years, there has been increasing concern, not only about the resource misallocations and inequities to which these redistributions give rise, but also about the resource misallocations to which the rent-seeking activities – the attempts by special interest groups to persuade the government to give them special treatment – give rise.[52]

In private contractual arrangements, issues of distribution arise, but they are limited: the only issue is how the surplus created by the transaction will be divided. Both must be better off as a result of the transaction – otherwise they never would have entered into it. What makes issues of distribution of such importance in the public sector is, I have said, the powers of compulsion, which allow the government actually to take away resources from individuals; moreover, virtually all public decisions have distributive consequences, both direct (for example, taxes) and indirect (taxes and expenditure programs may affect the *before-tax* distribution of income; some individuals benefit more from a public highway system, others from a public railroad system; each expenditure will have different consequences for different individuals). And what makes issues of distribution so difficult within the public sector is that, while almost all public decisions have distribution consequences, it is often difficult for the non-economist (or even the economist, for that matter) to tell what those distributive consequences are. Agricultural price supports may be argued for on the grounds that they deal with a market failure – the inability of farmers to insure adequately against the risks which they face; but a closer look at these programs reveals that that is not their true objective (indeed, in some cases, they may actually contribute to the risks faced by farmers) – they are really income transfer programs. (See, e.g. Newbery and Stiglitz, 1981.)[53]

Merit Goods

Merit goods have played a particularly troublesome role in traditional discussions of the role of government for several reasons.

Some merit goods arise from the State's acceptance of a redistributive role, and in particular from its role in providing social insurance. Any insurer attempts to monitor the actions of the insured, to ensure that the insured-against event does not occur. For one of the central problems of insurance is that, without monitoring, incentives to avoid the insured-against event are attenuated. If the government provides old-age insurance, against the risk of poverty, it is not unreasonable for it to require that individuals, while they are working, take prudential actions, that is, that they put aside savings for retirement in a relatively secure form. This is a justification for social security of some form (though again, not necessarily for government provision, only for the government to require that individuals make *some* provision for themselves).[54]

Some merit goods arise from the necessity of *someone* taking a paternalistic role with respect to children. The question is, should it be the child's parents or the State? There is a general consensus that young children should not have the right to decide whether to go to school or not. But who should make the decision? This question touches on fundamental philosophical issues which would take us beyond the scope of this paper.

But there is another set of merit goods. In some cases, they appear to be much like externalities, though they belong to a class of externalities which I sometimes call "spiritual" as opposed to "physical" externalities. There seems to me to be a fundamental difference between the externality which arises if I receive disutility simply from my knowledge of your drinking or smoking, and the externality which arises from my actually breathing your smoke. The appropriateness of the government using its powers of compulsion to intervene in spiritual externalities seems questionable at best.

Binding Commitments

Democratic governments have fundamental problems in making binding commitments.[55] The enforceability of contracts is generally recognized as central for the development of market economies. Without binding commitments (contracts), all transactions would have to be "spot," that is, only contemporaneous exchanges would be viable. Owners of a firm can, and do, making binding commitments, commitments which are binding not only upon them, but also upon their successors; when they sell the firm, the sale entails a transfer not only of the assets, but also of the liabilities, and included in the transfer are all the binding commitments. If current owners make commitments that a later owner may not like, it will be reflected in the price that the later owner will be willing to pay. Since the transaction is voluntary, when someone buys a firm, he willingly undertakes all the outstanding commitments of the concern.

But each government is sovereign. It may choose to recognize the obligations of a previous government, but it does so only voluntarily. In many (most?) societies, the government can only be sued "voluntarily," that is, it establishes the conditions under which individuals can attempt to recover funds from it; if it should decide that a particular class of contracts which it has signed are no longer binding, and if it further asserts that it cannot be sued for breach of contract, the insured parties have (at least in many countries) no further recourse.

And even should a government announce a policy of compensating for breach of contract, there are indirect ways by which contracts can be breached. It can, for instance, impose a tax which redistributes the rents arising from a contract.

The issue of contracts between the government and its citizens is, of course, broader than that of just commercial contracts. The social security system is often described as a contract between the government and the aged, and changes in the social security system are resisted as an unfair "breach of contract." (The contract between the government and the aged is, of course, nothing like an annuity insurance contract that an individual would purchase from a private firm.)

Though the government cannot make binding commitments, it can undertake policies (legislation) which affect the likelihood of different outcomes. Williamson has argued that governance structures matter, because they affect transactions costs. Once a piece of legislation is passed, there may be large transactions costs involved in reversing the policy. Though one government cannot commit a succeeding government, a government can make it more likely that certain commitments that it has made will be adhered to (and certain decisions it has made will not be reversed). Some have suggested, for instance, that the British Conservative government's strategy of ensuring that the shares of the privatized firms are widely distributed, and selling those shares at prices that were substantially below true market value, created a vested interest which makes a subsequent renationalization less likely. There is no binding commitment that those who buy shares in one of the nationalized firms will not have the property appropriated (just as there is no binding commitment that those who buy shares in any firm will not have their property appropriated). Still, the Conservative government's policy has made it less likely that even a subsequent Labour government would do so.

Thus the myriad of hurdles which a piece of legislation must pass (in the US, two houses of Congress, approval by the President, possible rulings by the Supreme Court) can be viewed as more than just a system of checks and balances: they constitute a form of commitment – once a piece of legislation is passed, reversing it is also difficult. The status quo thus has a special place.

Property Rights and Incentives

The importance of property rights for ensuring good incentives is now widely recognized. Renters have inadequate incentives to maintain the houses and apartments that they rent; farmers who rent land have inadequate incentives not to overgraze the land.

Businessmen build up their business partly with the intention of selling the going concern when they come to retire. In the absence of this ability to sell their firm, they would have no incentive in later years to maintain their reputation; they would run down the firm.

Managers of public firms have, in general, no way to appropriate the increase in value resulting from their managerial activities. Thus, not only are salary incentives limited, so too are the rewards which, in the private sector, take the form of capital gains.[56]

But it is, perhaps, wrong to say that managers in public enterprises have no property rights. They make innumerable decisions which affect the disposition of resources, and in that sense they do have property rights, though these rights are greatly constrained.

In many societies, the property rights that they do have can be turned into cash. Customs officials have the "property right" of allowing goods into a country. They can be (and in many cases are) richly rewarded for overlooking the importation of certain items which are either restricted or heavily taxed. Giving discretionary property rights almost invariably breeds corruption, particularly in poorer societies. This corruption is a major impediment to development in some less-developed countries.

In other societies, managers within the public sector earn returns on their property rights in non-pecuniary forms. The manager of one firm exchanges a favor (access to a rationed consumer good) with the manager of another.

In either case, the absence of property rights blunts long-run incentives, and the presence of limited property rights leads to distorted incentives.

To be sure, similar problems arise in the private sector. There is considerable evidence, for instance, that managers of private firms whose shares are widely held, who themselves own a small share of the firm they manage, engage in actions which are not in the interests of the firm. When such firms engage in take-overs, on average, the market value of their shares declines.[57] There are widespread complaints that managers pay too much attention to short-run profits (the basis on which they are rewarded) and not to the long run. Still, to the extent that managers' rewards are based on the stock market value of the firm, and to the extent that those market values reflect the long-run profitability of the firm, managers do take into account the firm's long-run interests.

This problem, like the preceding one, seems inherent in economic activity undertaken by the State. If the government vests a property right in an enterprise in its management, that is, gives them the right to sell control of the firm to another management team, then the government has basically "sold" the firm; it is no longer a state enterprise.[58]

Absence of Competition

Government is the sole organization in which membership is compulsory and which has the right to impose compulsory taxes. The government is, in this sense, a true natural monopoly.

But for some reason, when the government undertakes an economic activity, it seems to have a strong preference to be a monopolist, even when that monopoly is not necessary. (In this respect, it is perhaps no different from any other enterprise; what enterprise would not like to be a monopolist? The difference is not in the desire to be a monopolist, but in the ability to enforce one's monopoly position.) Thus, governments in most countries have maintained a monopoly over the post office (though the development of private express mail in the US has provided evidence that some competition is possible). Governments in many countries have maintained a monopoly over the telephone, though again, there is increasing evidence that, at least for some types of telephone service, competition is viable. Governments in many countries have only reluctantly allowed competition in TV and radio.

I would argue that there are many economic activities undertaken by the State for which competition is viable. Even if the government should decide to continue with the activity, little would be lost if entry was allowed.

There is one standard argument presented against entry: cream skimming. The entrant will provide, for instance, postal services in the major cities, leaving small towns unserved, or served only at high prices. Implicit in this argument is the existence of cross-subsidization: most economists' reaction to this cross-subsidization is that, in general, it gives rise to inefficiency (it distorts, for instance, patterns of location), and to the extent that there is a social interest in having more individuals living, for instance, in rural areas than would result from a free unsubsidized market, then such policies should be made explicit, and the costs of these policies made transparent. The government should provide the subsidy out of general revenues, not through an implicit tax on other users of postal services.[59]

Another objection is that it will result in unnecessary duplication, and hence allowing entry is economically wasteful. But if there are returns to scale, and the government is efficient, and if it prices at average costs, then entry will not be viable. Entry will occur only if the government is inefficient.

Competition is important for several reasons.[60] First, competition provides a basis of comparison. In the absence of competition, it is difficult to know whether a firm is efficient or not. How much should it cost to fly a plane between New York and Chicago? How much should a telephone call between those two cities cost? Most of us have no idea how to answer those questions. The only people who have the technological knowledge to answer such a question are those who run the firm. When there is only one firm, they will claim that they are being efficient, but how are we to evaluate their claim? The easiest, in some cases the only, way to evaluate such claims is by a comparison.

The comparison also provides a natural basis for incentives: reward structures which provide that the organization (individual) which performs better receives a higher income can provide strong incentives while imposing limited risks upon the contestants.[61]

There are incentives not only to produce efficiently and to innovate but also to produce the particular goods and services that individuals desire. For instance, individuals value their time. Firms that make customers queue up lose customers. Customers will be willing to pay more if they have to wait less in line. Firms will balance the extra revenues that they can receive from shortening queues with the extra costs of the required personnel.

Public bureaucracies seldom place a value on the time of their clients. While the costs of increased personnel to provide better service are apparent, and reflected in their budget, the benefits are not.

On the other hand, were two competing bureaus given the right to issue drivers' licenses, with a fixed fee given per license issued, the bureaus would be attentive to the kinds of services their clients desired.[62]

It is, of course, difficult to know precisely how much consumers value various services, and here again competition (and decentralization) has great advantages. Different communities will experiment with different kinds of programs. Some will be successful, some unsuccessful. But the spirit of competition will lead not only to more innovation, but also to more rapid diffusion of those innovations which prove successful.

It is the belief that competition will both improve efficiency and make public agencies more responsive to the needs of their clients that has been behind the voucher movement for public education. In these proposals, children would be given a voucher, to be used at any of a large number of competing schools meeting certain qualifications.[63]

More generally decentralized provision of public goods and services – having goods and services provided by local communities – provides the basis of competition among communities, the potential benefits of which were stressed by Tiebout (and a vast literature following upon his classic work).[64]

I suspect that there is a range of government services that can be provided in a more competitive way than they currently are.

PERSPECTIVES ON SOME CHARACTERISTICS OF GOVERNMENT

Critics of government have provided a long list of its vices: governments act inconsistently, they are inefficient, they are excessively conservative, they employ excessive red tape, etc. I have tried to argue that many of the problems facing government follow from some of its inherent characteristics, while others follow from characteristics commonly found (such as the absence of competition) but not necessarily inherent. In the following brief sections, we comment on how our framework provides some insight into several of the characteristics commonly associated with government.[65]

Red Tape

Government is often accused of paying excessive attention to following particular procedures. There are excessive delays with decision making. There is, in short, excessive red tape.

Some of these problems follow from the special fiduciary role that confronts government. Some of these problems follow from the difficulties associated with monitoring outputs of administrative activities – and ensuring that decisions are both good and fair. In the absence of judgments concerning output, the next best thing may be making sure that the process by which the decision was made was fair and thorough.

Finally, government administrators do not bear the costs of delay; they may partly bear the costs of mistakes; they do not bear the costs associated with consulting others. The incentive structure facing administrators is thus one which encourages red tape.

Awareness of the problem may help to mitigate it. Providing managers with time budgets may help. For some services, such as providing licenses, competition might be feasible and have significant beneficial effects.

Powerlessness and Conservatism

A complaint of those within government is that they feel individually powerless. A complaint of those outside the government is that the government seems powerless to deal with many of the social ills of society.

The distinctive strength of government – its universal membership and its powers of compulsion – are also its greatest liabilities. For as we have seen, these powers can be used to redistribute income, not only from the rich to the poor, but from the poor to the politically powerful.

Limited information implies that mistakes will be made. The mistakes that are made with concentrated power may be far more disastrous than those which arise in a society with decentralized decision making.[66] The more important the decision – the more significant the consequences of a wrong decision or the easier it is to make a wrong decision – the more limited will be the powers assigned to any individual; the decision will be made by a larger committee, requiring a higher degree of consensus (see Sah and Stiglitz, 1988). Thus, individuals can feel powerful, but only to the extent that they have power over unimportant decisions.

Finally, we have noted that those making decisions at one date may deliberately try to make it difficult to have their decisions reversed. The difficulty of making binding contracts leads them to design structures with high transactions costs for reversing decisions.

Thus, limited information, limited commitment abilities, and limited ability to prevent undesirable redistributions provide a natural set of explanations for the sets of checks and balances, the conservatism of political institutions, and the feelings of powerlessness of government and those within it.

This conservatism has its costs: institutions ossify, particularly when not subjected to competitive pressures. Change itself forces a re-examination of practices and procedures. Our analysis provides a rather different argument for privatization of public enterprises: it is not that privatization is necessarily better, but that the process of change will have beneficial effects. Our argument also provides a rather different explanation for the alternating emphases on the public and private spheres to which Hirschman called attention: the process of change itself may have value.

ECONOMIC POLICY

This essay has set forth the outlines of a Theory of the Economic Role of the State.[67] I have tried to define in what sense the State is different from other economic (and non-economic) organizations, and how these differences give rise to advantages, and disadvantages. I do not propose to consider in detail the implications of these general principles for any particular policy issue. Suffice it to say that I believe that some of the market failures are of sufficient importance that some form of government intervention may be desirable. The fact that government intervention is not perfect, that waste and incompetence may – or almost surely will – arise, should only remind us of the importance of human fallibility. Human errors arise in the private sector just as they do in the public. There is a difference – all of us have to pay for the mistakes in the public sector, while only the voluntary members (shareholders, workers, management) do in the private. This difference has its consequences, as we have emphasized: there are stronger incentives to avoid mistakes in the private sector than in the public sector. The management of the public sector is a public good, or as I sometimes put it, the Public Good is a public good. The focus of concern should not be the presence of mistakes, incompetence, and waste, but the differences in their prevalence. For some types of public intervention, the full costs of government intervention, taking into account the inevitable public failures, may be less than the benefits arising from correcting (or improving upon) market failure.

I am advocating here an eclectic position. Doctrinaire positions of the right, saying that government intervention at all times and in all circumstances is welfare-decreasing, that governments are inherently wasteful, that attempts at redistributions simply give rise to rent-seeking activities, are both wrong and unhelpful: governments will intervene when markets fail to meet social needs, and the economists' role is to guide them to understanding when and how government intervention is most likely to be helpful.

Similarly, doctrinaire positions of the left, calling for increased government intervention, idealizing the government, anthropomorphizing it as a single individual (a benevolent despot) and attributing the successive failures of government to correct the market failures to the particulars of the situation (e.g. to the particular leader of the government) without recognizing the limits of government, are also not very helpful.

The post-World War II period has led to a growing recognition of the inadequacy of what I shall call, for simplicity, these leftist positions. Nationalization of the basic industries in Britain did not lead to any qualitative change in the character of life in the country; it may only have led to a less efficient use of the country's scarce resources and to higher wages for those in the nationalized sectors. Socialism as an economic doctrine – the belief that simply by changing the nominal ownership of the means of production, or the means of production in certain vital industries, economic efficiency and broader social goals will be attained – is now dead.

What I fear, however, is that the inadequacies of the doctrines of the right will only gradually become apparent.

While I do not propose to assess the appropriate role of the government in any particular context, I wish to suggest several principles which can be derived from our analysis.

Monopoly

First, the government should be wary either of exercising monopoly power or granting monopoly rights (franchises). There are many circumstances in which natural monopolies arise, and in which government regulation *may* be desirable. But in these circumstances, when the incumbent is efficient, there is a natural barrier to entry: the government does not need to augment this with an exclusive license. Even if entry occasionally leads to duplication and waste, those costs are almost surely less than the benefits that potential (and actual) competition may bring.

Competition

Secondly, when possible, the government should encourage competition within the public sector. I am confident that the gains I detailed in previous sections (in incentives, in ability to identify relative competencies) outweigh any slight costs in duplication, or any slight waste arising from lack of coordination. (The problem is that the waste arising from duplication and coordination failures is often transparent. The waste from the lack of competition is not so transparent – it is more conjectural in nature: what costs would have been had markets been competitive.)

Decentralization

Thirdly, when possible, economic functions of the government should be decentralized. I have not, in this essay, undertaken an analysis of the advantages and disadvantages of decentralization. Though we conventionally think of government activity as centralized, it is in fact not an inherent property of state economic activity; and indeed, in the US (and many other countries) there is considerable decentralization of public economic activity. Much of it is undertaken by states and localities. Many of the arguments for decentralization parallel those given earlier for competition: decentralization allows a comparison of the performance of different localities (government bodies) in providing public services. Those communities which are well managed will be able to provide public services at lower costs (and hence lower taxes) than those that are less well managed, and thus will attract migrants, increasing property values.[68] The competition among communities thus services the same kind of roles that competition among firms does, not only in ensuring that the public goods that are provided are provided efficiently, but that the level and mix of goods accords well with the preferences of the citizens.[69] Decentralization has the further advantage of allowing a diversity of communities, accommodating to differences in preferences, and the competition among communities provides for incentives for communities to change, to adapt to changes in preferences and technology, and to innovate.

Decentralization thus provides a way for an "end run" around the problems posed by the equity constraint to which we referred earlier.

On the Economic Role of the State

Those who think that the community treats "unfairly" peo[ple for] their particular characteristics can move to another commu[nity.]

We have not yet thoroughly explored the range of decent[ralization] which is possible (or desirable) in the provision of goods and services by the State. The desirable degree of decentralization may well differ from service to service. There is little reason for fire-prevention activities to be provided at a "higher" level than the local community. There are a few instances in which coordination among the fire departments of different communities is required, but when it is, there seems no difficulty in eliciting the degree of cooperation required.

Education: An Example

Today, in the US, education is primarily the responsibility of local communities.[70] But recent arguments have suggested that further decentralization would be desirable.[71] The focus of control should be at the level of the school, rather than the school district. This would enhance parent and teacher participation in the school, improve the quality of education, and reduce administrative costs.

The central argument here for centralization is not coordination but equity: students going to different schools would receive a different education; some would, perforce, receive a better education than others.

(There is another argument, that because different schools would have different resource bases, the students at these different schools would receive different qualities of education.[72] But issues of control can, to a large extent, be separated from issues of finance: just as with a voucher scheme, the government can provide a uniform grant to all individuals to go to a qualified school,[73] so too can a central government provide uniform grants to member schools, requiring only that they adhere to certain minimum standards.[74] This makes clear that not only can the degree of centralization vary from activity to activity, but different aspects of the provision of a good and service – finance, employment, etc. – may be decentralized to different extents.)

The argument against decentralization is that the almost inevitable differences of treatment that would result would be unfair. This is an argument against local control of any state-provided good or service. The question is, what weight should be attached to these concerns about equity? Indeed, it is even possible that the gains in efficiency, innovativeness, and responsiveness resulting from decentralization and competition are sufficiently great that all individuals – even those who do "relatively" badly – are better off.

In those cases where there are private alternatives to publicly provided goods, there may not even be a trade-off between equity and efficiency concerns. Attempts to provide an excessively uniform public (state) education may lead to an exodus of the well-off from the public education system. Inequality may thereby be increased.

Though the State may have certain powers of compulsion, there is a general consensus that its powers of compulsion should be exercised only within limited domains. Individuals should be compelled to pay taxes. They may be compelled to fight in the armed services. They may be prohibited from opening up a competing postal service. But they should not be prohibited from sending their children to a private school, if they so choose. So long as there is a consensus concerning these limits on the government, there are limits on the extent of redistribution (the degree of equality in education received) that the State can enforce.

In many cases, however, we must admit that allowing more decentralization, more local control, will lead to some degree of inequality in treatment.[75] There are trade-offs. My judgment is that the gains from increased competition and decentralization would far outweigh the costs resulting from any slight decrease in equality. These are matters of values and judgments, concerning the returns to competition and decentralization.[76]

Other Advantages of Decentralization

There are several other advantages of competition and decentralization to which I wish briefly to call attention. I have stressed in my discussion the role that such competition has in improving efficiency. One aspect of efficiency (from the public perspective) is corruption: funds that are transferred from the public fisc, either directly or indirectly, to the benefit of public officials. If corruption in some community is greater than in others, its costs of providing services will be greater, and this will become reflected in tax rates.

I have also stressed the role of competition in making local service providers more responsive to the desires of their citizens, as well as the problems arising from the fact that the Public Good is a public good. For publicly provided private goods,[77] the consumers of the good or services have a strong incentive to monitor the quality, to ensure that the public service does what it is supposed to do. And even for more pure public goods, the individual's sense of efficacy is likely to be greater when the unit of organization is smaller. He is more likely to go to the trouble of exercising "voice" when things are not as they should be.[78]

Redistribution

Concerns about equity are pervasive in the public sector. We have seen how they affect both employment and expenditure policy. We have also seen that while they often provide the "rationale" for government policy, the redistributions are not those which would accord with generally accepted principles of equity; rather they are the consequences of special interest groups using the powers of the state to reap private gains at the expense of the general public. These redistributions are not only inequitable, but also inefficient. They are not only inefficient because of the rent-seeking expenditures that the special interest groups make in the quest for the special treatment; they are also inefficient because the equity constraint results in government programs that are ill-suited to any "rational" objective.

There is, alas, no way in a democratic society to proscribe such activities. There is no obvious way to distinguish these activities from more "legitimate" activities, e.g. providing information, remedying market failures. Severely limiting the scope of government activities, including those in areas where it has a "legitimate" advantage, may (probably will) reduce the scope for these special interest redistributions; but the price may be too high. As we have repeatedly emphasized, all systems, private as well as public, are marked by errors and imperfections. The fact that, in remedying market failures and redistributing income, some income gets redistributed to the well-off, and some inefficiencies get created, does not necessarily mean that the government programs should be eliminated. It only means that there is an added "cost" to the program which needs to be taken into account in judging whether it is worthwhile.

I suspect that bringing these redistributions out into the open will make them less likely to occur. The development of the Tax

Expenditure Budget in the US, showing how much various special provisions of the tax code were costing the Treasury, played an important role in the tax reforms which eliminated many of these special provisions. Developing a more comprehensive set of accounts, not only showing the magnitude of the costs and benefits, but providing alternative estimates of who were the beneficiaries (e.g. by income category), might similarly discourage the worst examples of these special interest programs.

Openness in Government

Throughout this paper I have emphasized the lack of incentives for, and the difficulties associated with, obtaining the kind of information required for good government, to ensure that good public managers are selected and that good public programs are designed, and to monitor that they are well executed. Information is a public good, and government has a responsibility to provide the requisite information and to lower the costs to others of obtaining what information they might judge to be relevant.

Several times within the past two decades, the American Congress has passed legislation trying to ensure that private firms provide the kind of information that consumers need to make good decisions. Lenders must report interest rates charged in a standardized way, and packages must be accurately labeled to reflect their contents. Yet Congress – and government more generally – has been loath to hold itself up to the same standards. One of the great advantages of the income tax is that individuals see what they are paying for government services. Yet Congress, in the tax reform act of 1986, shifted some of the burden to the corporation income tax, with misleading suggestions about who would bear the tax. With sales and value-added taxes, individuals never obtain a full picture of the taxes which they are paying.

There are similar problems on the expenditure side. The kinds of shenanigans employed by Congress to lower the (apparent) deficit – such as switching the day at which government employees were paid by a day, and several changes that were little more than accounting devices – might, had they been employed by a private firm, lead to charges of fraud and misrepresentation.

The failure of most governments to provide any hints of a capital budget – to distinguish investments from other forms of expenditure

– makes it particularly difficult to make judgments concerning public policy. No private firm could get away with simply reporting cash flows; it needs to indicate which of the expenditures are investments; it needs to present a balance sheet.

Nowhere are the informational problems more evident than when governments become involved in loan programs. In the US today, approximately a quarter of all lending (to the private sector) is either through a government agency or with government guarantees. This form of government program seems particularly attractive in times, such as these, when there are large deficits: the costs are not apparent – they only arise in the future when defaults occur. The magnitudes of the implicit subsidies and costs – both the total value, and who receives how much – are hidden.

Another category of government programs with hidden costs are government mandates – where government requires private firms, for instance, to provide health insurance for their employees. We have already referred to other instances: the costs of tariffs and voluntary export restraints are borne by consumers, but never show up in the government budget.

There are, obviously, incentives, both for some government officials and some special interest groups, not to have information of the kind we are calling for easily available. I noted in the beginning the importance of the appearance of equity. Programs are presented in a way which makes them seem reasonable. I suggested that the equity constraint is, in part, responsible for the peculiar form which some government programs take – they are designed to obfuscate who receives what benefits, because, were it more transparent, the program would be viewed as being inequitable.

I should note that in the US there has been progress in "truth in government." The tax expenditure budget was a major stride forward, and I suspect it played an important role in the attempted tax reform of 1986. The government has begun reporting regularly data concerning the loan programs, at least calling attention to this area of hidden expenditures. The Freedom of Information Act has made it considerably easier for citizens to obtain information about what the government is up to.[79]

But there are democratic governments who deliberately try to impede the flow of information – the Official Secrets Act in Great Britain stands in marked contrast to the Freedom of Information Act in the US.

TWO EXAMPLES

In the previous sections, I outlined a general theory and attempted to draw out from the theory some general lessons concerning economic policy. I have tried to illustrate the principles by examples – including an extended discussion in the previous section of education. Here, I wish to supplement that discussion with very brief and tentative reflections on two important government programs.

Government Retirement Programs

Most governments of the more developed countries have a retirement program with compulsory contributions. (In the US, it is generally referred to as social security, though, technically, the social security program includes several programs other than the retirement program.)

There are two alternative "justifications" for such a program: at the time they were enacted, there was a market failure, in that annuity insurance was not widely available; moreover, if the government is to assume a responsibility that all individuals have an adequate income in their old age, then it quite appropriately needs to compel them to make provision for their retirement.

But the social security program is more than an annuity (retirement insurance). It is a redistributive program, a redistribution across generations and within generations. Whether the program was designed to obfuscate these redistributions – to make it difficult for individuals to tell to what extent they had paid for what they were receiving – or not, it clearly has that effect.

Would individuals' attitudes towards social security be changed if they became more widely aware of these redistributions? Would middle-class retired Americans' attitudes change if they received a check amounting to half their retirement income labeled "welfare subsidy"?

Canons of good government – of what I referred earlier to as "truth in government" – suggest that the distinction between subsidy and insurance be drawn, not only in the government books, but also in the checks received by each individual.

Some critics of the social security system go farther: they say that we should allow private firms to compete with the government in providing for retirement insurance. (Clearly, the contributions to the redistributive components of the current social security system would have to be compulsory.) The government might have to set standards, to ensure that the funds are in fact being used to provide old-age annuities; but its over-riding interest in ensuring that individuals have made adequate provision for their old age could as well be served by private as public insurance. Passing over, for the moment, the potentially serious problems posed by adverse selection – that the private market would have an incentive to provide annuities to those with an expected short life – this seems to me a proposal which should be taken seriously. The government has an enormous advantage in transactions costs; in the US, the costs of administering the social security program are markedly less than those associated with most private annuity programs. Hence, apart from taking advantage of differential risks, I suspect that private firms might have a difficult time competing with the government, were it to provide retirement insurance on an actuarially fair basis. But the competition from the private sector might serve as an important discipline on the government.

Unemployment Insurance and the Human Capital Bank

Most developed countries also provide unemployment insurance. Again, the ostensible reason for this was a market failure: a risk against which the private market did not provide insurance (at the time).

The form which the unemployment insurance took was – from a theoretical viewpoint – peculiar. It insured against small risks – being unemployed for 26 weeks – a relatively small loss in the individual's lifetime income. What makes unemployment so painful, of course, is not the loss in lifetime income, but the inability of individuals to borrow to meet current needs. Thus the true problem was not a problem of insurance, but a problem of capital markets. And this problem is, at least partially, attributable to the difficulties banks have in collecting small loans.

The government is in an advantageous position. Its powers of compulsion make it easier for it to collect. Indeed, there have recently been proposals for education loans, with the repayments collected through the tax system. The tax system traces individuals as they move around the country. It is far more difficult to escape the net of the tax collector than to escape the net of the local bank. Government today has the facilities to keep track of loans and repayments made to individuals, not only for education, but also for temporary periods of unemployment.

This would have some distinct advantages over the current system. The current system has some marked adverse incentive effects. Individuals frequently wait until the 26th week of unemployment before getting another job – the incentive to work, or even to search for work, is greatly attenuated. If individuals could borrow, hardships would be avoided, and yet the individual would not have his incentives weakened.

CONCLUDING REMARKS

There is an important economic role for the State to perform. We have seen that the State can be viewed as an economic institution or organization with distinct advantages and disadvantages as compared to private, voluntary organizations. Some of the often noted differences are more matters of degree. Some of the differences are differences in practices, and changes, along some of the principles I have outlined, may reduce the differences in performance. Still other differences are inherent; they follow from the defining properties of the State, the universal compulsory membership, with the attendant powers of compulsion (to tax and redistribute), the attendant fiduciary responsibilities (with their consequences for employment and expenditure policy), and with the attendant limits, for instance on property rights and commitment abilities.

I hope that the perspectives presented in this essay will help inform not only the central questions concerning the balance between private and state economic activity, but also the equally important questions concerning the structure of state economic activity.

NOTES

1 Accordingly, the subject matter of this paper is immense, and I cannot do justice, either to it, or to the large literature addressing

the questions with which I am concerned here. I have chosen to focus my attention on certain aspects of the subject which, I think, have received insufficient attention. Thus, the limited space devoted to discussion of market failures does not reflect my judgment that they are unimportant, and, in particular, that they are less important than public failures. Rather, it simply reflects the fact that market failures are extensively and well discussed in the standard textbooks, while systematic treatments of public failures are only just beginning to make their appearance.

Similarly, the lack of attention to the role of government in stabilization (a role which follows from a particularly important set of market failures) should not be interpreted as meaning either that the government should not assume this role, or that this role is not important. Rather, it simply reflects my conviction that that is well-trodden territory, and while I think there still remains much of importance to be said on that matter, pursuing those topics would take us too far afield from the central issues on which I wish to focus here.

2   Throughout this paper I illustrate my points with statistics and examples drawn from the US. I do this because it is here that I have a comparative advantage. The problem of the role of government is, of course, universal, and I hope that non-American audiences will find the basic lessons I try to extract from these examples relevant and that seeing the problems from an American perspective will provide new insights into the specific issues confronting them.

One aspect of what is, I think, a particularly American perspective on government requires comment: the approach I take is quite ahistorical. I believe that studying how the roles undertaken by government have evolved is a very useful way of approaching an understanding of the issues. But the approach falls much more within the rationalist tradition. Assume we were, *ab initio*, to design the institutions of society. What would distinguish government from the other institutions? And what tasks would we assign to that institution?

As I shall comment below, the approach I take thus has much in common with the Theory of the Contract State, which seeks to understand the role of government as derived from the voluntary association of individuals. But that approach has not typically asked

how government differs from other voluntary associations, nor has it paid much attention to one of the distinctive properties of the State, automatic membership and subjection to its rules upon birth.
3 United Nations, *National Accounts Statistics, Government Accounts and Tables, 1983 Yearbook*, Country Tables 2, 3, and *Survey of Current Business* (July 1986), Table 3.14, cited in Stiglitz (1988a).
4 Musgrave seemed to believe that these represented three distinct activities, and that the analysis of each could be conducted separately from the others. Though we view the categorization as useful, it is only under special cases that the decisions are really separable. See Lau, Sheshinski, and Stiglitz (1978).
5 Though even here there are exceptions. Many rural communities have voluntary fire departments.
6 From Stiglitz (1988a). There are several ambiguities in the treatment of various categories of expenditures. National income accounting typically treats interest payments as transfers; we treat them as an expenditure on a factor of production (that is, capital services and labor services are treated symmetrically), allocated on a pro rata basis among other expenditure categories. Similarly, retirement (civilian and military) expenditures are sometimes categorized as transfer payments; we treat them as deferred compensation. At the federal level, there is some ambiguity about how to treat grants-in-aid to state and local governments; since for the most part these are tied to specific redistributive programs, we treat them as redistributive payments.

There are other reasons for caution in excessive reliance on these (or similar) statistics. Explicit subsidies to production are included as expenditures; indirect subsidies through the tax system are excluded. Traditionally, only the losses of government enterprises are included as expenditures, but, clearly, a quite different picture of the size and allocation of government expenditures would emerge if their total purchases of goods and services were included in expenditures, and their income included within government receipts. See Atkinson and Stiglitz (1980) for a further discussion of the difficulties of making comparisons across countries and over time.
7 Some have assigned an important role in the growth of government to the vested interests of politicians. This undoubtedly has

an important effect in the short run. When inflation coupled with the progressivity of the income tax yielded increased revenues to the government, the government quickly found uses for that money, at a time when it is doubtful that there would have been general approval of an explicit tax increase. Still, in democracies, governments are accountable to the electorate, and eventually they "speak out" – as they have repeatedly in the taxpayer rebellions, the most famous of which occurred in California, where a referendum limited the property taxes which local communities could impose.

8 Or lowered, depending on one's point of view: the government took the view that intervention should occur much more rarely than had previously been the case.

9 See, for instance, G. Stigler (1971).

10 The notion that potential competition can be just as effective as actual competition – firms will keep prices at low levels because, if they do not, entry will occur – is an old one, often associated with the Chicago school. See, for instance, Harold Demsetz (1968). A recent attempt at revival of this theory was led by W. J. Baumol; see, for instance, his presidential address to the American Economic Association (1982).

11 For potential competition to be effective requires very stringent conditions to be satisfied. Stiglitz (1988b) showed that even slight sunk costs could result in highly non-competitive outcomes.

12 A. Hirschman (1982) has put forward one explanation of what appear to be periodic shifts in the relative role assigned to government. To oversimplify this thesis: as individuals become disappointed with the failure of government to solve their problems, they turn to the private sector; but the disillusionment with the public sector is then followed by a disillusionment with the private sector.

13 In that sense, local communities are somewhat like a voluntary organization. As migration across countries becomes easier, the State's powers are diminished. For instance, one of the results of the literature on local public goods (Stiglitz, 1983a) with *costless* migration is that, if there is sufficient inter-community competition, there is no scope for redistribution by any one community. But, as I have emphasized elsewhere (Stiglitz, 1977, 1983a, 1983b), the assumption of perfect competition among communities

is even less credible than the assumption of perfect competition in conventional product markets, and to the extent that migration is costly and/or can be proscribed and competition among communities is limited, the State does have power over its citizens.

14 Hirschman (1970).

15 That is why the right to free emigration is important, putting a limit on the extent to which the government can abuse the rights of individuals and providing an open signal of popular discontent.

16 That is, the voluntary export restraints, under which Japanese firms have "voluntarily" limited exports to the US, have increased prices to consumers. Had a group of firms conspired to limit output, it would have been viewed as a violation of anti-trust laws. Here, we have the government doing precisely what the Japanese firms would have liked. (Quotas or tariffs might have had the same effect in limiting imports, but the revenues, in that case, could have accrued to the US treasury, rather than the Japanese manufacturers.)

17 Using the term in its more technical sense (Samuelson, 1954): a public good has two essential properties. It is costly to exclude an individual from its benefits, and it is undesirable to exclude an individual from its benefits, because the marginal costs of an additional individual enjoying the benefits of the public good are zero. Thus, defense is a public good: it would be virtually impossible to exclude anyone from the benefits of an effective national defense, and the cost of defense is virtually unaffected by the birth of an additional individual.

Good public management has both of these properties: all individuals benefit from an improvement in the quality of public management, and it would be difficult to exclude any individual from these benefits.

18 For the moment, we ignore the question of how important these elections are.

19 That is, if ownership is sufficiently concentrated, the difference in expenditures on information collection and processing concerning the quality of management if those spill-overs were taken into account and if they were not may be relatively small. This would be particularly true if most of the costs associated with ascertaining what is required of management and who are good managers were fixed costs.

20 In many instances, while the ownership claims on equity are widely diversified, debt is more highly concentrated. Thus, banks may exert more effective control than do shareholders, though the latter are nominally in control of the firm. There are again spill-overs to equity owners from these efforts on the part of banks. On the other hand, in some instances there are important conflicts of interests between lenders and owners of equity, a point which has long been recognized in the theoretical literature (Stiglitz, 1972), and which has been brought home forcefully by the highly leveraged mergers, acquisitions, and management buy-outs of the past decade. In countries where banks also own equity (such as Japan) these externalities may be partly internalized. See Stiglitz (1985) and Berle (1926).

21 There is a related problem in both public and private organizations: the characteristics which lead to survival within the organization may not necessarily be characteristics which lead to a high quality of leadership. Thus, within many modern large corporations, making one's way through the ranks often requires a set of social skills that have limited correlation with the innovativeness and creativity – or even the analytic skills which allow the identification of good from bad projects – which would have a large pay-off to the corporation. Similarly, the public relations skills required for success in public office may have only a limited relationship with managerial qualities.

22 In some cases, all that may be required is that management have a sufficient stake in the outcome. However, in some cases, managers may use their managerial discretion to allocate resources away from other shareholders and towards themselves. Managerial incentive schemes, without adequate monitoring, may not suffice. Thus, Shleifer and Vishny (1988) show that the expected return to firms engaging in take-overs is negative when management has a small stake in the firm, and the smaller the stake the more negative the return.

23 The difficulties of judging who are good managers and enforcing behavior which is consistent with the firm's interests are reflected in the econometric and events studies on the consequences of particular managers and managerial change for firm performance. While some studies (e.g. the classic one by Lieberson and O'Connor, 1972) indicate no effect on the firm's stock market

value when top management changes, others indicate a strictly positive increase when there is a change in management resulting from the death of the Chief Executive Officer.

24 North (1989) has noted this.

25 Many of the difficulties of public *and* private organizations arise from the difficulties not only of monitoring the actions, particularly of those engaged in administrative work, but also of judging which actions are undertaken for the interests of the organization and which actions are undertaken for the interests of the manager (see Hannaway, 1989). Managers have an interest to signal and broadcast their abilities, to entrench themselves within the firm, making themselves more indispensable and thus increasing their bargaining power, and to acquire skills which enhance their outside opportunities. These private interests are sometimes congruent, sometimes antithetical to those of the organization, but it is difficult for an outsider to separate out the two, let alone implement a contract which does so.

What economists have come to call principal–agent problems (Ross, 1973, Stiglitz, 1974a) are rampant in administrative organizations.

26 By the same token, management in industries with limited competition often seems to give in to wage demands on the part of the workers, paying them considerably above comparable workers in other industries, not because the increased efficiency of the workers warrants these higher wages, but because the increased contentment of the workers makes the task of management easier. The cost of the higher wages is borne by the shareholders.

27 I should emphasize, I am using the term "misappropriation" in a very broad sense. I am not just, or even mainly, concerned with those forms of misappropriation which can be and are prosecuted by the law. Rather, I am concerned with the multitude of minor misappropriations which are effectively unpreventable, e.g. paying a worker 10 percent more than his opportunity cost, or paying a firm 10 percent more for a product. No court could stop this: opportunity costs can be ascertained only imprecisely, and even then the manager might claim that it makes sense to pay workers high wages. It increases productivity and lowers turnover rates (and hence turnover costs.) There is almost always some hetero-

geneity of products (e.g. with respect to delivery times) and again the manager can claim it is worth it to pay the higher price, given the better delivery time, or the greater reliability of the firm, etc.

28 I do not want to suggest that, because it is difficult to ascertain what is fair, the concept of fairness is completely arbitrary and of no use in public policy decision making. My main concern here is to argue that the belief that public programs should be fair, and be perceived to be fair, imposes important constraints, constraints which are not imposed, or not imposed so forcefully, on other organizations. At the same time, we need to bear in mind both the important ambiguities in the concept, and the extent to which it is abused.

29 Pareto improvements are improvements which make some individuals better off, without making anyone worse off. Such changes are viewed to be unambiguously desirable, so long as society values outcomes in terms of how each individual is affected, and so long as an improvement in one individual's well being – keeping all other individuals unchanged – is viewed as socially desirable (even if the individual who is better off is the individual with the highest income, so that the policy increases inequality).

30 The problem posed by special interest groups is, in some ways, similar to the problem, discussed earlier, of distinguishing between managerial actions which are in the organization's interests and those which are in the interests of the manager. Special interest groups may claim that their function is to convey information (information will be undersupplied because of the Public Good associated with producing public good) concerning public decisions. And indeed, they are frequently in the position to be the best informed on the relevant issues.

31 The branch of economics which is concerned with making statements concerning what government (or society) *should* do, and with understanding what kinds of assumptions (concerning, for instance, values) are needed to make such statements.

32 Elsewhere, we have provided a criticism of the view that all that is required is potential competition. See Stiglitz (1988b).

33 This is not to say that there is anything like the perfect competition that characterizes the standard competitive equilibrium model.

34 See, for instance, Stiglitz (1982a).

35 Daves and Christensen (1980).
36 That is, the problems of ensuring that managers act in the interests of the organization.
37 For a more extensive discussion of these issues, see Stiglitz (1989). For a discussion of the role of relative performance schemes as incentive devices, see, for instance, Lazear and Rosen (1981) or Nalebuff and Stiglitz (1983).
38 In the traditional competitive paradigm, banks have no distinct role in allocating capital, other than as an intermediary. In our economy, banks perform a central role in screening among loan applicants, and thereby allocating capital.
39 See Coase (1960).
40 There is some disagreement about what precisely merit goods are. A simple working definition which will suffice for our purposes is: merit goods are goods that the government compels individuals to consume or use, like seat belts and elementary education, out of concern by the government that individuals might not, without such compulsion, act in their own best interests. Merit goods and bads involve the government taking a paternalistic role; they represent an abandonment of the principle of consumer sovereignty, which holds that each individual is the best judge of what is in his own best interests.
41 Indeed, whether the market economy is or is not constrained Pareto efficient may depend on the distribution of wealth, as Shapiro and Stiglitz (1984) demonstrate.
42 For informational reasons, as explained below.
43 For textbook expositions at the elementary level, see Stiglitz (1988a), and at the more advanced level, see Atkinson and Stiglitz (1980).
44 Sappington and Stiglitz (1987b), p. 569.
45 We do not enquire here into either the reasons for those constraints, or their desirability – or into the question of whether similar constraints should be imposed on the government.
46 And even this statistic may underestimate the transactions costs, since it does not take into account the fact that since premia are paid prior to the payment of benefits, there may be a considerable accrual of interest.
47 In a more general context, this is a point made by Salop and Stiglitz (1977, 1982).

48 Some of the economic costs are not direct expenditures, but rather arise from provisions of the insurance contract (deductible and co-insurance clauses). See Rothschild and Stiglitz (1976).
49 These informational problems have been at the center of the literature on optimal taxation during the past two decades. See Mirrlees (1971), and Atkinson and Stiglitz (1980). More recently, I have focused attention on *Pareto-efficient tax structures*, that is tax structures which have the property that no one can be made better off, without making someone else worse off, taking into account the information constraints faced by the government (what are sometimes called the incentive compatibility constraints). See Stiglitz (1982b, 1987).
50 It may, however, still be constrained Pareto efficient (to use the vocabulary of the previous note), taking into account the informational constraints. See Stiglitz (1977, 1982b).
51 Our earlier caveat concerning limits on the extent of redistribution that can be imposed if there is free migration and competition among communities should, however, be recalled.
52 A. Krueger (1974) and others have recently emphasized the importance of rent-seeking, the expenditures of those attempting to get favorable treatment in persuading the public and the politicians (bribes) to grant them those favors. Thus, in the US the expenditures of the milk lobby to retain the high prices at which they have been supported have attained a certain notoriety. In less developed countries, bribes to obtain tariff protection are allegedly common. Rent-seeking is obviously important. I suspect, however, that the argument that all of the rents are dissipated in rent-seeking activities – that there is, as a result, little gain in redistribution, but just a resource misallocation – is probably not true. (The traditional arguments concerning rent-seeking are, in some ways, similar to the arguments in the contestability literature that potential competition will ensure that prices will be driven down so low that profits will be zero. Recently, Stiglitz (1988b) has shown this conclusion to be wrong, if there are any sunk costs. The incumbent can charge a high price, make large profits, and still deter entry. By the same token, an incumbent – a current receiver of rents – need not spend all of his rents to maintain his position within the public largess.)

53 It should be clear that ignorance – well intentioned but misguided policies – may play as important a role as the attempt of special interests to divert resources to their own uses. Thus, the popular support for the corporation income tax is based on the fallacy that the burden of the tax rests with the "corporation" – and, if not there, with rich stockholders.

54 But there may be transactions costs advantages of having the government provide the social insurance.

55 Actually, in practice, non-democratic governments face similar difficulties. They can pretend to make a commitment that is binding either upon themselves or on a later government, but there may be little that those who are harmed if the government subsequently abrogates its commitment can do.

56 These property rights even play an important role in those activities where it is difficult to write explicit contracts, and where accordingly greater reliance must be placed on reputation mechanisms. The "good will" of a firm is an asset; maintaining the value of that asset provides the owner of a firm with incentives just as the owner has incentives to maintain the firm's physical assets. See, for instance, Eaton (1986).

57 Shleifer and Vishny (1988) have a more extensive discussion of the evidence that managerial and firm incentives do not coincide.

58 Though these are matters partly of definition, and one could imagine a variety of mixed cases of granting management limited property rights.

59 There is a slightly more sophisticated version of this argument: when there are increasing returns to scale, some commodities will have to be priced in excess of marginal costs. The optimal set of prices (called Ramsey–Boiteux prices) may entail a high price on some commodity (one whose compensated price elasticity is low). At that price, entry will be viable. Thus, social welfare will be higher if the government could set its prices without worrying about the constraint imposed by the threat of entry.

No government has, in fact, implemented a set of Ramsey–Boiteux prices; the information required for its implementation is in general not available; the prices are very sensitive to the precise values of the own and cross-elasticities; the welfare losses associated with imposing, say, a uniform set of mark-ups are, by most accounts, small; and, in particular, in the presence of an (optimal) income tax, uniform mark-ups may in fact be optimal.

For a more extensive discussion of these issues, see Sappington and Stiglitz (1987a) and Stiglitz (1987).

60 It will be noted that the sense in which we are using "competition" is quite different from that embodied in the standard Arrow–Debreu model of the competitive market. Our use of the term is much closer to the ordinary use of that term (e.g. sports contests), and to the use of that term by Schumpeter.

61 See Lazear and Rosen (1981) and Nalebuff and Stiglitz (1983). The latter also show that contests have the important property of incentive flexibility, that is, the level of incentives is adjusted automatically in response to the nature of the environment. When the task to be performed is easier, efforts adjust to take this into account.

62 The equity constraint imposes further distortions on government behavior in the absence of competition, which competitive pressures would help ameliorate. There might be a public outcry if rich individuals were deemed to get "preferential" treatment (faster service) simply because they were willing to pay more.

63 This is not the occasion to provide a detailed discussion of the advantages and disadvantages of vouchers in education. For a more extensive discussion, see, for instance, Levin (1980). Voucher schemes for education face particular problems arising from concern about the social stratification to which they might give rise, from imperfect information on the part of parents, who are making choices for students, and from limited competition – most students would probably choose to go to their neighborhood school in any case. The GI bill for higher education can be viewed as a voucher scheme (generally considered quite successful).

64 Tiebout's classic paper (1956) has spawned a huge literature, attempting to ascertain the conditions under which competition among communities provides Pareto-efficient outcomes. The conclusion of this literature is that the conditions required are far more stringent and less likely to be satisfied than those required for the efficiency of markets for conventional private goods. See Stiglitz (1977, 1983a). For a survey of some of the more recent literature, see Stiglitz (1983b). For textbook discussions, see

Stiglitz (1988a), chapter 26, and Atkinson and Stiglitz (1980), chapter 17.

65 I do not comment on one characteristic – the seeming inconsistency of governments – which receives considerable popular comment, not because it is unimportant, but because it has been dealt with extensively elsewhere in the literature. Government decisions are not made by a single individual, but are made collectively, and there are strong reasons to believe that such social choices will not have the kinds of consistency properties associated with individual decision making (Arrow, 1951).

66 For a more thorough analysis of the consequences of alternative organizational structures for the nature of the decisions made, see Sah and Stiglitz (1985, 1986).

67 I should emphasize that I have not attempted to construct a comprehensive theory. I have not, for instance, discussed the role of the government in economic stabilization, either the sources of market failure, which give rise to the need for government intervention, or the instruments by which such interventions might best be effected. Nor have I addressed the particulars of government intervention in any of the areas in which market failures arise.

68 This assertion has to be qualified: it depends to some extent on the true incidence of the taxes and expenditures. If much of the incidence of the tax lies with landowners, who represent a minority of the voters, then there may be little incentive for economic efficiency. If expenditures are reflected in rents and taxes are not, and the median voter is a renter, then in fact there will be little incentive for economic efficiency and possibly perverse incentives with respect to expenditures (Stiglitz, 1988a). The implications of this for the design of voting and tax structures remain an unexplored question.

69 This important insight is generally attributed to Tiebout. Just as competitive markets for private goods lead to Pareto-efficient outcomes only under restrictive conditions (the absence of market failures), so too competition among communities leads to Pareto-efficient outcomes only under restrictive conditions. The required conditions are, however, far more restrictive and less likely to be satisfied than those required for private goods. Indeed, some of

the implications for the structure and performance of local communities, were those conditions satisfied, are sufficiently peculiar (e.g. there would be unanimity on all political issues, all workers of a given type within a community would have the same preferences) as to raise serious doubts about the optimality of decentralized provision of local public goods. Tiebout's insights, however, concerning the virtues of competition remain I think germane. Moreover, our earlier comments that the presence of market failures need not imply the desirability of government intervention remain equally applicable here: central government intervention to correct the inefficiencies of decentralized provision is likely to have its disadvantages, no less than government intervention to correct private market failures.

70 For non-American readers, a brief description of the organization of the American elementary and secondary educational system may be useful. Responsibility for education lies primarily with local school districts (towns, cities, counties, depending on the location). These school districts hire the principals of the schools (the headmasters) and exercise considerable control over the schools. Curricula, for instance, are generally determined by the school district. Funding is largely through local property taxes, with significant and increasing contributions coming from the states. While the State allows considerable local autonomy, it imposes a number of requirements (e.g. length of school day, age at which children may leave school, mandating certain courses). The states have taken an increasingly active role, in many areas, for instance, requiring schools to select textbooks from an approved set of textbooks. The federal government's role is quite limited. It provides, for instance, support for certain disadvantaged children.

The role of the courts is limited to ensuring that certain constitutional guarantees are adhered to, but these constitutional guarantees have been increasingly broadly interpreted. Thus, California's state constitution has been interpreted as guaranteeing a certain degree of equality of educational expenditures, and it is on this basis that caps on the expenditure of richer communities have been imposed.

71 See, for instance, Hannaway (1988).

72 We are ignoring for the moment Coleman's finding (and the

controversy to which it gave rise) that there is no significant relationship between the quality of education and the level of educational expenditures.
73 Defining what is a "qualified" institution will, of course, entail a limited degree of centralized control.
74 There is, of course, always the danger that in setting these minimum standards, the centralized authority will seek to exert more than a minimal amount of centralized control.
75 I have, perhaps, understated the problems associated with redistribution when goods and services are locally provided. In the extreme case of the Tiebout model, when financing is completely local, no redistribution is feasible. On the other hand, fiscal equalization schemes which give communities autonomy over their level of expenditures invariably have distortions; the marginal cost to the community of spending an extra dollar may be more or less than a dollar. See Coons, Clune, and Sugarman (1970), Feldstein (1975), and Stiglitz (1974b, 1977, 1988a). The importance of these distortions depends, of course, on the price elasticity.

I would argue, however, that even if one abandoned local autonomy on the level of expenditure, decentralization and competition would have distinct advantages.
76 In this discussion of education, I have focused my attention on how, if government is to be involved in education, it might be most effective. I have not addressed the prior question of why government should be involved; that is, is there a market failure which can account for government having a role. Elsewhere, I have suggested that there are, in modern developed economies, limited externalities; that is, at the level of education which individuals would demand in their own private interests, the gains to others from further education of any particular individual are, at best, limited. For a more extensive discussion of this issue, see Stiglitz (1988a), chapter 15, or Lott (1987).
77 Publicly provided private goods are goods, like education, which could, in principle, be provided privately; it is relatively easy to charge for the goods and the marginal cost of an additional individual enjoying the good is significant.
78 The relationship between organizational size and participation is a question with which sociologists have been concerned.

A related advantage arises in providing motivation (incentives) for workers. Group incentives seem to be effective in small groups, possibly because of peer monitoring. Of course, large organizations can be organized with small worker groups; again different aspects of an organization may be organized with different degrees of centralization.

The efficiency gains from this kind of monitoring have recently been discussed by Arnott and Stiglitz (1988).

79 In my own research into government programs to sell oil and gas leases, I have found the act extremely useful.

REFERENCES

Arnott, R. and J. E. Stiglitz (1988), "Dysfunctional Social Institutions," NBER Working Paper no. 2666.

Arrow, K. (1951), *Social Choice and Individual Values*, Cowles Commission Monograph no. 12 (New York: Wiley).

Atkinson, A. B. and J. E. Stiglitz (1980), *Lectures in Public Economics* (New York: McGraw-Hill).

Baumol, W. J. (1982), "Contestable markets: An uprising in the theory of industry structure," *American Economic Review* (March), pp. 1–15.

Berle, Adolph A., Jr. (1926), "Non-voting stock and 'bankers' control," *Harvard Law Review*.

Coase, R. H. (1960), "The problem of social cost," *Journal of Law and Economics*, 3, pp. 1–44.

Coleman, James, T. Hafer, and S. Kilgore (1981), *Achievement in High School: Public and private schools compared* (New York: Basic Books).

Coons, J. E., W. H. Clune, and S. D. Sugarman (1970), *Private Wealth and Public Education* (Cambridge, MA: Harvard University Press).

Dasgupta, P. and J. E. Stiglitz (1988), "Potential competition, actual competitive and economic welfare," *European Economic Review*, pp. 569–77.

Daves, D. W. and L. R. Christensen (1980), "The relative efficiency of public and private firms in a competitive environment: The case of Canadian Railroads," *Journal of Political Economy*, 88, pp. 958–76.

Demsetz, H. (1968), "Why regulate utilities?," *Journal of Law and Economics*, 11, pp. 55–66.

Eaton, Jonathan (1986), "Lending with costly enforcement of repayment and potential fraud," *Journal of Banking and Finance*, 10, pp. 281–93.

Farrell, J. (1987), "Information and the Coase Theorem," *Journal of Economic Perspectives*, vol. I, no. 2.

Feldstein, Martin (1975), "Wealth neutrality and local choice in public education," *American Economic Review*, vol. LXV, no. 1, pp. 75–89.

Greenwald, B. and J. E. Stiglitz (1986), "Externalities in economics with imperfect information and incomplete markets," *Quarterly Journal of Economics* (May), pp. 229–64.

Hannaway, Jane (1988), "Decentralization and education," Vice-presidential address delivered to the American Educational Research Association, Washington, DC.

Hannaway, Jane (1989), *Managers Managing: The workings of an administrative system* (Oxford University Press).

Hirschman, A. O. (1970), *Exit, Voice and Loyalty: Responses to decline in firms, organizations, and states* (Cambridge, MA: Harvard University Press).

Hirschman, A. O. (1982), *Shifting Involvements: Private interest and public action* (Princeton, NJ: Princeton University Press).

Krueger, A. (1974), "The political economy of the rent-seeking society," *American Economic Review*, vol. LXIV, no. 3, pp. 291–303.

Lau, L. J., E. Sheshinski, and J. E. Stiglitz (1978), "Efficiency in the optimum supply of public goods," *Econometrica*, 46, pp. 269–84.

Lazear, E. and S. Rosen (1981), "Rank order tournaments as optimum labor contracts," *Journal of Political Economy*, 89, pp. 841–64.

Levin, H. M. (1980), "Educational vouchers and social policy," in James Guthrie (ed.), *School Finance Policies and Practices: The 1980's* (Cambridge, MA: Ballinger).

Lieberson, S. and S. F. O'Connor (1972), "Leadership and organizational performance: A study of large corporations," *American Sociological Review*, 37, pp. 117–30.

Lott, John R., Jr. (1987), "Why is education publicly provided?," Working Paper, Hoover Institution, Domestic Studies Program.

Mirrlees, J. A. (1971), "An exploration into the theory of optimum income taxation," *Review of Economic Studies*, 38, pp. 175–208.

Musgrave, R. A. (1959), *The Theory of Public Finance* (New York: McGraw-Hill).

Nalebuff, B. and J. E. Stiglitz (1983), "Prizes and incentives: Towards a general theory of compensation and competition," *Bell Journal of Economics*, vol. 14, no. 1.

Newbery, David M. and J. E. Stiglitz (1981), *The Theory of Commodity Price Stabilization* (Oxford: Clarendon Press).

North, D. (1989), "Institutions," *Journal of Economic Perspectives* (forthcoming).

Nozick, R. (1974), *Anarchy, State, and Utopia* (Oxford: Basil Blackwell).

Ross, S. (1973), "The economic theory of agency: The principal's problem," *American Economic Review* (May), pp. 134–9.

Rothschild, M. and J. E. Stiglitz (1976), "Equilibrium in competitive insurance markets: An essay on the economics of imperfect information," *Quarterly Journal of Economics*, vol. XC, no. 4, pp. 629–49.

Sah, R. K. and J. E. Stiglitz (1985), "The theory of economic organizations: Human fallibility and economic organization," *American Economic Association Papers and Proceedings*, vol. 75, no. 2.

Sah, R. K. and J. E. Stiglitz (1986), "The architecture of economic systems: Hierarchies and polyarchies," *American Economic Review*, 76, pp. 716–27.

Sah, R. K. and J. E. Stiglitz (1988), "Committees, hierarchies, and polyarchies," *The Economic Journal*, 98, pp. 451–70.

Salop, S. and J. E. Stiglitz (1977), "Bargains and ripoffs: A model of monopolistically competitive price dispersions," *Review of Economic Studies*, 44, pp. 493–510.

Salop, S. and J. E. Stiglitz (1982), "The theory of sales: A simple model of equilibrium price dispersion with identical agents," *American Economic Review*, vol. 72, no. 5, pp. 1121–30.

Samuelson, P. A. (1954), "The pure theory of public expenditure," *Review of Economics and Statistics*, 36, pp. 387–9.

Sappington, D., and J. E. Stiglitz (1987a), "Information and regulation," in E. Bailey (ed.), *Public Regulation* (London: MIT Press), pp. 3–43.

Sappington, D., and J. E. Stiglitz (1987b), "Privatization, information, and incentives," *Journal of Policy Analysis and Management*, vol. 6, no. 4, pp. 567–82.

Shapiro, C. and J. E. Stiglitz (1984), "Equilibrium unemployment as a worker discipline device", *American Economic Review*, vol. 74, no. 3, pp. 433–44.

Shleifer, A. and R. W. Vishny (1988), "Managerial entrenchment," paper presented to conference at Princeton University.

Stigler, G. (1971), "Theory of regulation," *Bell Journal of Economics* (Spring), pp. 3–21.

Stiglitz, J. E. (1972), "Some aspects of the pure theory of corporate finance: Bankruptcies and take-overs," *Bell Journal of Economics*, vol. 3, no. 2, pp. 458–82.

Stiglitz, J. E. (1974a), "Incentives and risk-sharing in sharecropping," *Review of Economic Studies*.

Stiglitz, J. E. (1974b), "Demand for education in public and private school systems," *Journal of Public Economics*, 3, pp. 349–86.

Stiglitz, J. E. (1975), "The theory of screening, education and the distribution of income," *American Economic Review*, vol. 65, no. 3, pp. 2283–300.

Stiglitz, J. E. (1977), "The theory of local public goods," in M. S. Feldstein and R. P. Inmen (eds), *The Economics of Public Services* (London: Macmillan).

Stiglitz, J. E. (1982a), "Ownership, control, and efficient markets: Some paradoxes in the theory of capital markets," in K. D. Boyer and W. G. Shepherd (eds), *Economic Regulation: Essays in honor of James R. Nelson* (Ann Arbor, MI: Michigan State University Press).

Stiglitz, J. E. (1982b), "Self-selection and Pareto efficient taxation," *Journal of Public Economics*, 17, pp. 213–40.

Stiglitz, J. E. (1983a), "Public goods in open economies with heterogeneous individuals," in J. F. Thisse and H. G. Zoller (eds), *Locational Analysis of Public Facilities* (New York: Elsevier–North-Holland), pp. 55–78. NBER Reprint 433.

Stiglitz, J. E. (1983b), "The theory of local public goods twenty-five years after Tiebout: A perspective," *Local Provision of Public Services: The Tiebout model after twenty-five years* (New York: Academic Press, Inc.), pp. 17–53. NBER Reprint 489.

Stiglitz, J. E. (1985), "Credit markets and the control of capital," *Journal of Money, Credit, and Banking*, vol. 17, no. 2, pp. 133–52.

Stiglitz, J. E. (1987), "Pareto efficient and optimal taxation and the new New Welfare Economics," in A. Auerbach and M. Feldstein (eds), *Handbook of Public Economics* (Amsterdam: Elsevier–North-Holland), pp. 991–1042.

Stiglitz, J. E. (1988a), *Economics of the Public Sector*, 2nd edition (New York: W. W. Norton).

Stiglitz, J. E. (1988b), "Technological change, sunk costs, and competition," *Brookings Papers on Economic Activity*, 3, 1987, M. N. Baily and C. Winston (eds), Special Issue on Macroeconomics (Washington, DC: Brookings Institution).

Stiglitz, J. E. (1989), "Incentives, information, and organization design," *Empirica* (forthcoming)

Tiebout C. (1956), "A pure theory of local expenditures," *Journal of Political Economy*, 64, 416–24.

Part II

Comments

Comments 1

Mark Perlman

The Special American Meanings of the Word "Government"	90
The Fin-de-siècle Growth of Governmental Intervention	93
The Background	93
The Situation after the Civil War	94
Adams's Formulation of the Principles of Governmental Intervention	94
Commons's Distinction between "Government-in-Industry" and Industrial Government	95
The Post-World War II Debate	98
Some Comments on Stiglitz's Formulation	99

Professor Stiglitz has offered his treatment of an old problem. His perspective is that of an American currently in the field of public economics.[1] My perspective comes from experience as an economic historian writing in the field of the history of economic thought. Hence, what I offer initially is in large measure simply background material essential for non-Americans reading about the American experience; it contains some points not consistent in assumption with Professor Stiglitz's statement about the sovereign power of government in America.

I do, however, want to consider other features of Professor Stiglitz's interpretation, which relate his work to earlier American efforts in the same field. And I close with comments on some aspects of Professor Stiglitz's essay which suggest that some new ground is being broken.

My comments, then, follow three avenues:

1. Explanation of certain special interpretations Americans almost automatically put on the word "government."
2. Indication of the American intellectual legacy in interpreting the optimal role for governmental intervention.
3. Placement of the Stiglitz argument in an historical framework.

THE SPECIAL AMERICAN MEANINGS OF THE WORD "GOVERNMENT"

There is an unfortunate lacuna at the beginning of Professor Stiglitz's approach, one which becomes serious when he identifies government with full, rather than limited sovereign, power. He assumes that "government" is a noun stemming from the verb "to govern". American history, however, is replete with qualifications of this semantic transformation. The American constitutional experience has been one long effort to bound or to limit this simple syntactical shift.

When the present American republic was in its earliest stages, a self-conscious decision was made to put on the Great Seal of the United States the phrase *Novus Ordo Saeculorum*. What did the Founding Fathers have in mind, and why did they believe that they were creating an entirely new concept of the relationship between the governed and the government? And what has subsequently happened? I suggest several things:

(1) They thought that the overall government of the American federation was to derive its *limited*[2] authority from the majority of the electorate – it was to be, as President Lincoln put the matter almost 100 years later, when he apparently emphasized not the preposition but its object as the key word in the three phrases, "government of the people, for the people, and by the people." Lincoln's has proven to be hardly an empty sentiment, because it means that the struggle to keep the civil servants from running society has been in the national consciousness for over 100 years, at least. Whatever deviations have been introduced over the past 201 years by misguided practice, the principle of "equal justice under law and no preference given to the governing group" (certainly almost a novel proposition in 1787–8) has had profound effects on what the American federal government is supposed to be doing. In sum, then, one explicit element in the American federal governmental system has been an overwhelming prior commitment to a representative, limited, republican principle of self-government, with most elected officials, whether they realize it or not, likely to be relegated to the side lines long before they have thought the game was over.

(2) The fear of the abuse of governmental power was so great that when the federal system was sketched the already limited powers of

that government were intentionally further weakened by trifurcation. Because the powers of many Western-style governments all over the world have since that time been divided (usually by bifurcation), many Americans often overlook the point that their process of trifurcation represented an unusual change. Conscious of the parliamentary tyranny during the English Commonwealth (1649–60), the American Founding Fathers were fearful of excesses within the legislative process and sought to offset such by separating and making co-equal the powers of the executive, in this instance the presidency. Within less than a generation (1803), the leading federal court would unilaterally arrogate to itself the authority to decide what was *ultra vires* for each of the two other branches. It is true that the Founding Fathers' decision to separate the chief executive from the Congress has been partly undermined by the practice of making the chief executive the nominal leader of his party (cf. Agar, 1950), but even with such derived influence, whether his party has or has not controlled either or both houses of the Congress, American presidents have far more frequently than not been unable to control the congressional legislative process. Division of limited powers as it exists within the American federal government is a far more devastating limitation on the governmental process than any underlying economic efficiency principle could be – jealousy between the two non-judicial branches serves to cripple, if not to paralyze, the decision-making power. Such was the original intent, and such is the way events have generally worked out.

(3) The powers of the federal government are specifically enumerated in the federal Constitution; those not listed are essentially non-existent. Principally the listed ones relate to intra-national (more than one state) and international trade. Only after the crucial 1937 *Jones–Laughlin* decision was the federal government permitted *in normal peacetime* to intervene in matters affecting working conditions, wages, and maximum hours without the payment of penalty rates. Previously these and many other matters (health and certain kinds of factory legislation, the normal police powers (maintenance of order), checking of weights and measures, registration of vital statistics, etc.) were either reserved to the states or *ultra vires* – the usual prohibition of such standards-setting was associated with the "full freedom to contract" provisions of the 5th and (post-Civil War) 14th Amendments.[3] Decisions authorizing federal, state, and local governmental intervention into matters of racial discrimination first surfaced in the

early 1950s; and when they did the courts seized upon a loophole in the legal process and declared unilaterally that certain contractual provisions such as racial covenants in real-estate titles were unenforceable, because they were in the view of the Supreme Court "contrary to the public purpose." This post-World War II decision laid the modern groundwork for a kind of creative judicial intervention into areas where the Congress had been politically unwilling to tread.

Put in a nutshell, American legal and political history has been, is, and likely will continue to be littered with problems of *the absolutely necessary* constitutional authorization for matters affecting the government–free market–individual citizen relationships. "By what constitutional authority?" is no small matter for Americans seeking governmental help to solve social problems. Generally reliance has, since 1937, been put on the Interstate Commerce clause, which reserves to the federal government the right to regulate anything that is shipped over state borders.[4]

It is often believed that the federal government is the only one that matters within the American society. Such a conclusion is not warranted; the state and local governments control the schools, the police and fire protection systems, most of the road construction and maintenance, most of the health protection systems, including water and sewage disposal (but not the health of most retired workers), etc. Each state government relies for its explicit authority on its own state constitution, and it generally does not derive its explicit powers from the federal government, although almost from the beginning no state law was permitted (accepted as constitutional) by the federal courts if it was in conflict with the federal Constitution, and more recently if it was in conflict with a policy which the Congress had the right to define and had moved to no action – even if that right was seemingly shared with the states.[5]

Local governments derive their authority from state constitutions and laws specifically enacted by the state legislatures. Again, what I seek to emphasize is that not only has the historical effort been to make governing by the federal trifurcated government difficult, but a parallel effort has been to make state and local governments weak.

One other important point remains to be made. If the constitutional process served to make the various levels of political government weak, from the very beginning the philosophical intent of the Founding Fathers was to make the right of free association close to paramount. Business enterprises were favored, and by the mid-1840s working men not only had political suffrage, but their claim to the right to form unions was almost general. Government in the US may have commonly meant the politically selected instrument, but in practice associationism quite aside from the formally selected bodies had great power, surely not absolute power, but in many instances as much power as did the so-called sovereign entities.[6] Thus it is that I find Professor Stiglitz's view that government has compulsive powers somewhat greater in Platonic theory than it is in Aristotelian fact. True it is that Chief Justice Marshall, *while cutting back the power of the states*, observed that "the power to tax is the power to destroy," but nonetheless "the power to tax" is one which the electorate traditionally considers dangerous – as the Democrats in this past decade are beginning to realize.

THE FIN-DE-SIÈCLE GROWTH OF GOVERNMENTAL INTERVENTION

The Background

Prior to the American Civil War (that is, prior to 1861) there had been so much regional friction within the Congress that efforts to pass internal improvement acts generally came to nothing. In 1860, however, Abraham Lincoln ran on a platform intended to bind together politically the free-states of the Middle West, California, and the northern free-states. He promised *inter alia* to sponsor legislation offering free, inalienable, small (160-acre) tracts of land for family farming (it was termed "homesteading"), federal subsidies for a transcontinental railroad *through Chicago*, and protection for domestic manufacturing industry. These promises were fulfilled, and if the railroad was built corruptly (and so it seems it was) it was built quickly, and, according to Professor Robert Fogel's intriguing book (1960), economically from the social standpoint.

What Lincoln did not promise in his election platform was a concerted policy relating to credit and monetary expansion and control. The purported reason was not constitutional; seemingly it dealt with regional differences between the industrialized and creditor Northeast and the rural and debtor Midwest.

The Situation after the Civil War

Lincoln's election clearly precipitated the Civil War and by the time that war was over, and Lincoln had been assassinated, there had been under Lincoln's assertion of the Executive's "war powers" massive federal intervention into virtually all elements of economic activity. The Secretary of the Treasury and the Congress had expanded the currency supply with unbacked paper money, and there had been a wartime federal income tax (something seemingly explicitly prohibited under the "peacetime" Constitution).

Time and space preclude reviewing carefully what happened during the third part of the nineteenth century, but by the 1890s there was strong populist[7] political pressure, emanating from a set of "market-marginal" states forming something of a half-circle stretching from the Dakotas and Minnesota in the North through Nebraska, Kansas, and on eastward to Alabama and Georgia in the South. One major element of populist focus was concerted state and federal legislation to redress the economic power balance which the railroads, it was held, dominated. First the states, and then the Congress, seemingly obliged. Whether these acts, including the derivative Sherman and Clayton Antitrust Acts, were seriously meant to do anything is a topic about which many have written (cf. Witte, 1932, pp. 66–74, 168–70). Suffice it to say, that the legislation reflected some degree of political power and a great amount of public anger.

Adams's Formulation of the Principles of Governmental Intervention

One of the many academics who tried towards the end of the last century to formulate some principles relating to governments coming to grips with the "new economic situation" was Henry Carter Adams, a longtime Professor of Economics at the University of Michigan. Adams, for many reasons an important (if currently unsung) figure in American academic history, was the one who organized the specific objectives and policies of the Interstate Commerce Commission, which was the Congress's initial effort at intervention into railroad control through regulation.

Adams, one of the first PhDs in economics (Johns Hopkins, 1878), took immediately afterwards some post-doctoral training in

Bismarckian Germany and was greatly influenced by experimentation in legislatively authorized social reform occurring there. He returned to America with a mind turned from the virtues of laisser-faire. In time he wrote many seminal essays on the relationship between government and economic factions within the citizenry. Two are particularly relevant to our understanding of Professor Stiglitz's topic: "The State and Industrial Action," given before the Constitution Club and the Institute of Social Science in New York City in March 1886, and his Presidential Address before the American Economics Association in December 1896 (see Adams, [1886, 1896] 1954).

Adams clearly had no attachment to the principles and/or the ideology of laisser-faire. He thought, perhaps along the lines of John Stuart Mill's writings, that governmental intervention freed as well as confined, created as well as destroyed.

What Adams wrote was that there existed a presumptive case for governmental intervention (and it could be along any of the various lines that Professor Stiglitz suggests on pp. 57 of his essay) if,

1. There is a need to establish "planes of competition," by which Adams clearly meant minimal standards relating to product and particularly to factor market competitiveness.[8]
2. Firms, like established railroads, are producing under monopolistic conditions of increasing returns, such that large firms are inevitably able to undersell smaller firms.[9]
3. The launching of a successful enterprise involves such large, indivisible inputs that activity could not commence without some form of governmental guarantee. These indivisibilities involved all of the inputs – and although Adams did not and/or could not spell out the then unpublished Boehm–Bawerkian contribution of understanding the determinants of the length of the period before the necessity for profits began to show and had to be realized and/or paid (time being the major aspect of the contribution of the capital share), this point was probably implicit.[10]
4. Economic redress is essential to the preservation of social harmony.[11]

Commons's Distinction between "Government-in-Industry" and Industrial Government

Another academic working in this field was John Rogers Commons, Professor of Economics at the University of Wisconsin from 1903 until his retirement in 1932. Like Adams, Commons wrote extensively on the problems of regulating industry, but his approach, perhaps an antecedent to Professor Stiglitz's, focused on the problems of civilizing and stabilizing the developments in industry. These goals involved what Commons called a choice between government-in-industry (by government he meant federal, state, and local political intervention, using all of the means Professor Stiglitz mentions on p. 40) and "industrial government," something not necessarily involving any forms of legislative, executive branch, or judicial branch action.[12] Commons was likely America's most experienced academic hand at drafting the kinds of economic legislation designed to do just those things which Professors Adams and Stiglitz thought must be done,[13] but he had doubts about the efficacy of civil servants trying to take on and successfully control the principal actors in the governance game; his view was that the reforming governmental commissions were either likely to be captured by those who were to be the subject of reform, or the coalition which created the reforming commission once the legislation was passed would fall apart and the commission would become something like Chinese "paper tigers" (cf. Bernstein, 1955, 1972). Commons urged two things; first, that the major economic parties be encouraged, with the help of experts,[14] to formulate their own *open* agreements, and that the role of the government (federal or state) be limited to enforcing rules of openness. Second, that the parties eschew governmental assistance lest it rob them of their necessary organic creativeness and will-to-life (cf. Perlman, 1984).

Commons advocated a form of cartelization, something seen in the bilateral relationships between labor unions and employer federations, and also in their contacts with likely consumer groups – any self-defined interest bloc which had the desire and either the market or political power to gain a chair at the bargaining sessions. Covenants, as I have indicated, had to be worked out openly, and if outrages surfaced and persisted, Commons, following the argument offered by James Madison in the *Federalist Paper, No. 10*,[15] believed that those adversely affected or insulted would be encouraged to develop a countervailing public influence.[16] Commons had more faith in the essential reasonableness and wisdom of the leaders of powerful economic groups *when made to take responsibility in the open* and when they were challenged to deal directly with their opposites than he had in the capacity of civil servants, usually inflexible in approaching the different value systems one finds in the market place, to control events over the opposition of those same leaders. Such had been his experience in Wisconsin, and he thought it could be generalized (Commons, 1919; Commons, [1921] 1969; Commons, [1934] 1964; Commons and Andrews, [1916, 1920, 1927] 1936). One should add that Commons seems to have expressed relatively little concern about the parties enforcing their covenants on individuals; what Professor Stiglitz refers to as Albert Hirschman's "right to exit" – exactly what Locke meant when he described the individual's right to freedom (escape from one community to another) – was in Commons's estimation supposed to solve any difficulties.

Commons had considerable suspicion of unscrupulous economic blocs getting control over government bureaucrats, with the two then running amok: *quis custodiet ipsos custodes* ("who will police the policemen?") was no minor question in his seminar, just as it must have been among those with whom Adam Smith had regular discourse. Smith's answer was in theory, at least, the eschewing of powerful government administrations (mercantilist in nature) and in part open disclosure. Commons followed Smith in this regard; where they differed was in Commons's conviction that small competitive units could not survive and invariably led to oligopolistic arrangements. Commons was no populist/anti-monopolist (Commons, [1934] 1964). To the four economic tests I have ascribed to the Henry Carter Adams approach, Commons offered some additional considerations. Governments should intervene when

5   Market competition clearly cannot be controlled by the interested parties coming unassisted to bilateral agreement *and when in their frustration they ask the public authorities to help in the resolving of standards-setting.*[17]
6   The market system, with all of the impersonality associated with price competition, cannot assure individuals of protection against such hazards of modern economic life as superannuation, unemployment, industrial accidents including death, and catastrophic illnesses. And in these instances it is technically necessary for reasons of "spreading the risk and cost" to adopt universal social security coverage. But even here Commons's view was that it was optimal where possible to fund the system in such a way as to

reinforce the individual employer's and the particular union's propensity to "look after his/its own."

The Post-World War II Debate

During the interwar period the debate over the efficacy of socialism and public ownership of the means of production was conducted on two levels. The political socialists fared badly; their high-water mark on the national scene had been earlier, in 1912, when their presidential candidate, Max Hayes, gained more than a million votes. And the advent of the Roosevelt New Deal, designed to revivify the private sector, gave little comfort to those who favored public ownership, although there were major exceptions in the area of electricity generation. These exceptions fell within several of the exempted areas suggested by both Professors Adams and Commons.

On the academic plane, the socialists fared better. There was continual discussion in the professional literature about the feasibility of socialism, with one or more levels of government using the political process to make economic decisions. The argument was not American in origin; I would cite Nicolaas Gerard Pierson (1902), Enrico Barone (1908), and Ludwig von Mises (1920) as the framers of the original phase on whether socialism could use the free market's pricing system (cf. Lavoie, 1985, reviewed in Perlman, 1986). Professor Fred Taylor of the University of Michigan argued in 1929 that use of marginal adjustments could make the socialist pricing system feasible. Taylor's argument was restated in an improved form in 1936 by Professor Oskar Lange (of the University of Chicago, no less). But, it was Beveridge's 1944 *Full Employment in a Free Society* and Hayek's 1944 *The Road to Serfdom*, both popular reading during World War II, which launched the postwar heated discussion. And Lerner's 1944 *The Economics of Control: Principles of welfare economics*, as well as John Maurice Clark's 1948 *Alternative to Serfdom* and his 1949 *Guideposts in Time of Change*, fleshed out differing opposing approaches.[18]

My point is that the post-1980 materials cited by Professor Stiglitz have a long and even honorable past, and aside from the American institutions-minded, like Adams and Commons, there was a debate flourishing.

SOME COMMENTS ON STIGLITZ'S FORMULATION

Professor Stiglitz's approach is concerned almost exclusively with two considerations. What is efficient and what is equitable? The question of efficiency embraces efficiency of production, efficiency of administration, and, implicitly, efficiency of consumption. What is equitable is harder to handle because it involves what is meant by equitable, who determines what is meant, and who bears the inequitable costs of the solutions. And while he draws from the literature some concepts such as property rights (hardly the stuff of equity) and public goods and bads (again empirically not the kinds of things which generally serve achievement of equity – as he himself notes), he offers efficiency as the alternative to what can be called ideology. Comparative efficiency, he asserts, is a persuasive answer to socialism.

One particularly valuable point he makes early in his essay is that various recent *observed* experiences with inefficient and corrupt governmental mismanagement are not conclusive.

I think that his efforts to identify equity-achievement are most important. And while I favor "semantic discipline" and recognize that equity is an economist's word-of-art, I think that the phrase "priorities of redistribution and group preference" is what would make Professor Stiglitz's position original and particularly relevant. For it is the achievement of certain particular definitions of equity which the market does not seem to be able to achieve.

As I have noted, I do not find compelling the Stiglitz view that central planning of production and distribution can be judged on grounds of efficiency. What is compelling is that economies work within national or international institutional frameworks, and underlying those frameworks are ideological preferences. Where I find the Stiglitz interpretation particularly useful is in his stressing that the tie between equity claims (what I would prefer to call "priorities of redistribution and group preference") and the varieties of means of control is changing its shape as new economic needs surface.

I dare not end without adding that, if the issue remains in no small part ideological, treating it as such serves little use. Some three centuries ago the forerunner of modern secularism, Pierre Bayle (who came to live in this very city, Amsterdam), argued that since religious wars were not proving conclusive, perhaps competitive prayer might. It would, he noted, cause a good deal less bloodshed. He even suggested that prayer for one's enemy could be more cost-efficient than trying to convert or kill him had been. Better that the socialists/planners and free market enthusiasts should pray than try to convert each other. But, reverting to an efficiency test just does not seem to me to grab either.

I suggest that the six points in the legacy of Adams and Commons offer a clear understanding and persuasive case for explaining under what circumstances governments (public or private, as in the Commons case) should move to center stage. What Stiglitz adds is the point that the tilting of preferences (what he calls "equity") is the way that ideology is now getting its share of the limelight. Perhaps for the present it is hard to drum up enthusiasm for central plannng; yet, as Stiglitz clearly concludes, that seems, even now as we confer, the only way for the poor to get economic security.

NOTES

1 Many Americans reading this book will be unaccustomed to the phrase "public economics," but it is an appropriate one. Originally I described Professor Stiglitz as a specialist in public finance, a category which I adopted for the classification system used in the *Journal of Economic Literature*. Like many economics subfields, public finance suggests different things to different people. The American academic economics profession has generally considered tax codes not to be at the heart of their interest. Rather, in years past the public finance specialists have concentrated on the efficiency and equity involved both in tax collecting and in governmental spending. By and large, some of these emphases have significantly changed since the publication in 1944 of Abba Lerner's *The Economics of Control*, and in 1959 of Richard Musgrave's *The Theory of Public Finance*, and the contemporaneous development of the economic subfield, macroeconomics. Recent emphasis had included among other things governmental policies concerned with income (and employment) maintenance, the conditions requisite to economic growth (raising per capita income levels), economic equity (diminishing dispersion of intra-population income levels), and price stability. The question of who

owns the means of production had usually been confined in the interwar period to the academic subfield of comparative economic systems, although such Austrian School and Austrian School-influenced economic theorists as Mises [1920] and Hayek (1944) wrote extensively on the topic. "Public economics" is a fine phrase used to describe this myriad of fiscal controls and questions of who owns, controls, manages, and polices, and who thinks about governmental economic policies, and I am truly grateful to Professor Heertje for suggesting it to me as a substitute for "public finance."

2 Several of the Founding Fathers (delegates to the constitutional convention in 1787) were conversant with John Locke's work on constitutional government; all were experienced with George III and his ministers' abuse of the prerogative, which had led to the American Revolution and the Declaration of Independence in 1776.

3 Until about 1911 the federal Supreme Court struck down all state efforts to pass factory legislation. Thereafter, some factory acts were passed and upheld in the courts, but they touched on matters of health and accidents; wage- and hour-regulation was under the 5th and 14th Amendments precluded – either for the state or the federal government. The 1937 decision, already mentioned, was the forerunner of a similar decision upholding the rights of the states to regulate hours and wages, and the federal act setting these standards was first passed in the next year (1938).

4 There is one exception. When the 18th "Prohibition" Amendment was repealed, its replacement (the 21st Amendment) permitted states the right to regulate commerce in intoxicating beverages.

5 The federal courts have usually but not always held that once the Congress has debated and declined to pass a legislative remedy for a matter within any purview of the congressional authority, even if a state chooses to pass legislation designed to affect that same matter the federal decision to eschew legislation binds the state's hand.

6 Churches, fraternal lodges such as the Freemasons and the Knights of Columbus, and special interest groups, even if regularly condemned by most of the organs trying to shape public opinion, have long histories of quasi-compulsive authority.

7 The classic populism of the Brothers Gracchi is only partly the model for American populism. Traditionally, rural American populism, supported by small "petit bourgeois" farmers, sought policies offering low interest rates, low transportation costs, and the sale inexpensively of state- and federally-owned lands. More recently there has been a development of urban populism – the constituency of the Reverend Jesse Jackson is only among the latest to embrace this form of populism. It includes racial minority groups, the poor, and to some extent those who advocate cheap public housing and an increased number (relative and absolute) of public goods suited to the impecunious.

8 This is the freedom of association or the right to organize or the labor unions case, involving a justification for workers combining to raise wages, set safety-on-the-job standards, etc. Mr Justice Oliver Wendell Holmes Jr. thought that syndicates or associations not only could not be kept from organizing, but that their organization was the hallmark of free men.

9 This is the natural monopolies case.

10 This case has many faces. Sometimes it involves governmental subvention of private firms undertaking internal improvements (e.g. canals, railroads) when the pay-off period was too long to make profitable what were deemed socially necessary projects. Other times, as in the case of Eli Whitney's development of the principles of mass-production in his fabrication of standard-part rifles, it involves governments encouraging what Boehm–Bawerk termed "roundaboutness" in the expectation of introducing newer and better technology, with the assumption that unit prices would be lower. Or, it could involve governmental regulations discouraging too-short time horizons for figuring profits – as in the current "après moi le déluge" habits of aging corporate executives, who want the corporate balance sheet to look profitable during their time at the helm. These examples pertain to the capital market; others could pertain to human capital investment as well – as in the instances of governmental subvention of training and research.

11 If this was once mainly the American form of an historic rationale explaining the judicial reinterpretation of the anti-combination laws (that is, laws concerning the formation of labor unions), more recently it has become the rationale for all sorts of redistributive legislation. The Webbs' Method of Collective Bargaining, once

the preferred American instrument for redistribution, has given way to their Method of Legal Enactment. Yet, as the American colloquialism goes, "the party is not over until the fat lady sings"; the explicit thrust of the Reagan presidency was to thwart the drift towards governmentalism. What the new Bush Administration will seek is at the time of this writing unclear; the language seems to suggest hewing to the Reagan official line of less rather than more federal government.

12 Commons reflected the influence of the Pragmatists – an American philosophical school, probably inspired by the philosopher William James, who argued that in addition to everything else a good idea had to be capable of successful application. John Dewey, a leader of that school, argued in a 1926 set of lectures, *The Public and its Problems*, that voluntary group-engineered decisions were the "natural" way to solve group problems (Dewey, [1927]). That kind of voluntarism had great appeal to Commons ([1934] 1964).

13 Among other things Commons helped draw up the first Workman's Compensation Act (Wisconsin, 1911) the operation of which secured court approval, the first comprehensive factory act permitting a State Commission to prescribe constantly rising minimum working environment standards (Wisconsin, 1911), the first public utility act permitting discriminatory rate-setting, the first authorization of a centralized budget office within American government (Milwaukee), and the first Unemployment Insurance Act (Wisconsin, 1931).

14 Cf. Charles Merriam's dictum "experts on tap, not on top."

15 Madison's point, written to persuade the voters of New York State to accept the federal Constitution, was that the remedy for one group's grasp for power was to set up countervailing groups, or split the dominant faction, or a bit of both.

16 Commons was one of the earlier strongest advocates of countervailing power; indeed, there is little in John Kenneth Galbraith's treatment of the topic in the 1950s, 1960s, and 1970s that he himself does not admit to Commons having said earlier (Galbraith, 1958, 1967).

17 Commons's classic example dealt with the resolution of the post-World War I railroad strike. Eventually the two massive parties (managements and the railroad brotherhoods) worked out a jointly agreeable solution involving a legislative proposal for the

Congress to enact. It became law and resolved the difficulties – that solution lasted for almost four decades (cf. Richberg, 1930).
18 There are several elements in the early phases of this debate: Enrico Barone's, Nicolaas Gerard Pierson's, and Ludwig von Mises's essays reappeared in Hayek (ed.) (1935); and the Taylor and Lange essays were reproduced in Lippincott (ed.) ([1938] 1964). Abram Bergson wrote an evaluative summary in Ellis (ed.) (1949). A highly condensed version of the issues as well as the references can be found in Perlman (1986).

REFERENCES

Adams, Henry Carter ([1886, 1896] 1954), *Relation of the State to Industrial Action, and Economics and Jurisprudence: Two essays by Henry Carter Adams*, ed. with an introductory essay and notes by Joseph Dorfman (New York: Columbia University Press).

Agar, Herbert (1950), *The Price of Union* (Boston: Houghton Mifflin).

Barone, Enrico ([1908]), "The Ministry of Production in the collectivist state," in Hayek (ed.) (1935), pp. 245–90.

Bergson, Abram (1949), "Socialist economics," in Howard S. Elllis (ed.), *A Survey of Contemporary Economics* (Philadelphia: Blakiston), pp. 412–48.

Bernstein, Marver (1955), *Regulating Business by Independent Commission* (Princeton: Princeton University Press).

Bernstein, Marver (special ed.) (1972), *The Government as Regulator, Annals of the American Academy of Political and Social Science*, vol. 400 (Philadelphia: American Academy of Political and Social Science).

Beveridge, William (1944), *Full Employment in a Free Society* (London: Allen & Unwin).

Clark, John Maurice (1948), *Alternative to Serfdom* (New York: Vintage).

Clark, John Maurice (1949), *Guideposts in Time of Change: Some essentials for a sound American economy* (New York: Harper).

Commons, John Rogers (1919), *Industrial Goodwill* (New York: McGraw-Hill).

Commons, John Rogers ([1921] 1969), *Industrial Government* (New York: Arno).

Commons, John Rogers ([1934] 1964), *Myself: The autobiography of John R. Commons* (Madison: University of Wisconsin Press).
Commons, John Rogers and John B. Andrews ([1916, 1920, 1927] 1936), *Principles of Labor Legislation* (New York: Harper & Brothers).
Dewey, John ([1927] 1954), *The Public and its Problems* (Denver: Swallow) ["This volume is the result of lectures, delivered during the month of January, 1926, upon the Larwill Foundation of Kenyon College, Ohio."]
Fogel, Robert William (1960), *The Union Pacific Railroad: A case in premature enterprise* (Baltimore: Johns Hopkins Press).
Galbraith, John Kenneth (1958), *The Affluent Society* (Boston: Houghton Mifflin)
Galbraith, John Kenneth (1967), *The New Industrial State* (Boston: Houghton Mifflin).
Hayek, Friedrich A. von (ed.) (1935), *Collectivist Economic Planning*, reprinted 1975 (Clifton, NJ: Augustus M. Kelley).
Hayek, Friedrich A. von (1944), *The Road to Serfdom* (Chicago: University of Chicago Press).
Lange, Oskar (1936), "On the economic theory of socialism," in Lippincott (ed.) ([1938] 1964), pp. 55–143.
Lerner, Abba Ptachya (1944), *The Economics of Control: Principles of welfare economics* (New York: Macmillan).
Lippincott, Benjamin E. (ed.) ([1938] 1964), *On the Economic Theory of Socialism* (New York: McGraw-Hill).
Mises, Ludwig von ([1920]), "Economic calculation in the socialist commonwealth," trans. S. Adler, in Hayek (ed.) (1935), pp. 87–103.
Musgrave, Richard Abel (1959), *The Theory of Public Finance: A study in political economy* (New York: McGraw-Hill).
Perlman, Mark (1984), "Governmental intervention and the socio-economic background," in Gold, Bela, et al., *Technological Progress and Industrial Leadership* (Lexington, MA: Lexington Books), pp. 609–31.
Perlman, Mark (1986), "Review of Donald Lavoie, *Rivalry and Central Planning: The socialist calculation debate, reconsidered*," *Market Process*, vol. 4, no. 1 (Spring 1986), pp. 4–6.
Pierson, N. G. (1902), "Het waardeprobleem in een socialistische maatschappij" [The problem of value in a socialist society], *De*

Economist, pp. 423–56; Eng. trans. in Hayek (ed.) (1935).

Richberg, Donald Richardson (1930), *Tents of the Mighty* (New York, Chicago: Willett, Clark & Colby).

Taylor, Fred M. ([1929]), "The guidance of production in a socialist state," in Lippincott (ed.)([1938] 1964), pp. 41–54.

Witte, Edwin Emil (1932), *The Government in Labor Disputes* (New York: McGraw-Hill).

Comments 2

Douglass C. North

What has been the Economic Role of the State?	108
What should be the Role of the State?	109
What is it Feasible to Expect of the State?	110

The questions that I believe should be addressed to deal with the issue of the economic role of the State are: (1) What has been the role of the State? (2) What should be the role of the State? and (3) What is it actually feasible to expect the State to do?

We learn what has been the role of the State from our knowledge of the past – from economic history, as well as the evidence accumulated on political-economic relationships in the current world. What should be the role of the State entails specification of positive criteria of allocative and adaptive efficiency and normative criteria of equity and the trade-offs between efficiency and equity. To determine what it is possible for the State to do entails modeling the political process so that we may develop realistic criteria of political performance rather than rely on strictly normative considerations that may be – and usually are – outside the choice set of the political actors. To model the political process we must re-examine the behavioral assumptions we use with respect to both the motivation of the actors and the complexity of the problems to be solved (and the consequent implications for the processing of information). Equally it is necessary to analyze the exchange process between political and economic institutions. Let me enlarge on each of the questions I have posed in the light of Professor Stiglitz's essay.

WHAT HAS BEEN THE ECONOMIC ROLE OF THE STATE?

Throughout most of history the State has not provided a framework conducive to economic growth. Indeed the Mafia would be a more accurate characterization of the State in the past than an organization concerned with "the public good." There were of course exceptions. We think of civilizations in Mesopotamia, Egypt, Greece, and Rhodes, and the Roman Republic and Empire. But they were exceptions; and a State that is self-consciously concerned with the performance of the economy is a relatively modern phenomenon, dating from the mercantilist era but probably more accurately associated with the rise of "representative" government.

The emergence of representative bodies in the polity resulted in a system of organized exchange between rulers and those constituents with the wealth and income to be taxed. The context was the growing cost of warfare in late medieval Europe that was first described by Joseph Schumpeter in "The crisis of the tax state" (1954). Rulers, desperate for additional revenue, (reluctantly) gave up some authority to the Parliament, Estates General, or Cortes in return for levies or ultimately taxes. The resultant process of exchange led to a broader concern with the health of the economy; constituents could and did press for a curb on the sovereign's authority over the economy but with widely varied consequences (depending on the outcome of the ubiquitous struggle for control between the "representative" bodies and the Crown).

In Spain the ultimate consequence was repeated bankruptcy, arbitrary confiscation of assets, and three centuries of relative stagnation. It was also a set of political-economic rules which, carried over to Latin America, have been (and continue to be) an underlying cause of the relatively poor economic performance and political instability of the countries in that Continent.

In England, in contrast, Parliament effectively shackled the powers of the sovereign in 1689, created a structure of relatively efficient property rights and credible commitment by the polity that resulted in the rapid development of the capital market, and paved the way for the long-term growth of the economy.[1] These rules were carried over to the New World and are responsible for the relatively good performance of the North American countries in comparison to those in Latin America.²

Now I raise these historical issues not as antique curiosities but because they have significance for our time. Economists (such as Professor Stiglitz) ordinarily take for granted a state that has created a set of rules of the game that are broadly conducive to economic growth. But not only are such rules still the exception, as politics in the Third World give ample evidence, there is no guarantee that they will be perpetual even in the developed world, as the modern history of Argentina attests. Indeed I contend that the central and most difficult role of the State is to establish and enforce a set of rules of the game that broadly encourage the creative economic participation of all of its citizens.

WHAT SHOULD BE THE ROLE OF THE STATE?

An ideal polity would be concerned with the range of issues that Professor Stiglitz discusses in his paper: fiduciary responsibilities, equity constraints, market failures (both public and private), etc. But for an economic historian concerned with the long-run viability of economies, such a wish list, fine as far as it goes, is still incomplete. I am equally concerned with the adaptive efficiency of economies, which is different than the standard allocative efficiency criteria of the economist. Of necessity adaptive efficiency is derived from a set of political-economic institutions. It is concerned with the tolerance of a society to the acquisition of knowledge and learning; to a society's encouragement of innovation, risk-taking, and creative activities of all sorts. The encouragement, via the appropriate institutional framework, of trials, experiments, and innovation, is essential because in a world of uncertainty no one knows the "correct" answers to the problems we confront – as Alchian (1950) pointed out many years ago.

Different institutional rules will produce different incentives for the acquisition of knowledge, for learning by doing, and for the selection of trials to be undertaken. The rules will not only determine the kinds of economic activity that will be profitable and viable (productive versus redistributive activities, for example). They will also shape the adaptive efficiency of the internal structure of firms and organizations via rules that regulate entry, governance structures, and the flexibility of organizations. In particular rules that encourage the development of tacit knowledge and therefore creative entrepreneurial talent will be important (Nelson and Winter, 1982).

Professor Stiglitz has an excellent discussion of two conditions essential to adaptive efficiency: competition and decentralized decision making. He also makes a case for the importance of property rights for incentives. One must, however, take the discussion further than he does because the property rights important for allocative efficiency are not altogether coincidental with those important for adaptive efficiency. Property rights and political rules that provide the most secure protection to current forms of economic activity may discourage innovation or alternative forms of economic organization. There is nothing new about this issue, as Professor Stiglitz is well aware, but it does have important implications for what is possible, the subject of the next section of my comments.

Finally, adaptive efficiency entails the elimination of errors. Bankruptcy laws accomplish this objective in the private sector in developed economies. The problem of eliminating mistakes is in the public sector. Without competitive pressures to force their elimination, government rules, regulations, programs, and agencies multiply. Their survival, perpetuation, and multiplication is all too seldom a reflection of their success in solving problems. The structure of rules, therefore, is not only one that rewards successes but also one that vetoes the survival of "inefficient" activities and organizations. A major dilemma of modern polities is establishing and enforcing criteria of adaptive efficiency both in the private and public sectors. To do so we must understand how polities work.

WHAT IS IT FEASIBLE TO EXPECT OF THE STATE?

In this section I wish to argue that you cannot get there from here. "There" is the ideal polity discussed in the preceding section; "here" the neo-classical framework that is the foundation of economic analysis. You cannot because:

1   the implicit model of the polity that most economists have is

inconsistent with the behavioral assumptions underlying economic theory;
2 when we build a model of the political-economic system employing those behavioral assumptions we cannot get the desired results discussed by Professor Stiglitz and explored on pp. 109–10 above. But since we do have political-economic systems that (however imperfectly) do manage to realize many of those objectives, something is missing in our models.

Let me explore each of these issues in turn.

(1) Traditionally economists have been content to give politicians good advice and have assumed that the politicians could accept and act upon that advice. That is, they have generally told politicians what would be an efficient solution to a political-economic issue. For longer than I can remember we have been telling politicians that tariffs are bad; for even longer than that politicians have been ignoring our advice. In the post-World War II era of Keynesian persuasion, advisers to US presidents told them to run budget deficits in periods of unemployment and economic slack and budget surpluses in periods of full employment and inflationary pressure. The presidents obliged with the deficits, period. What made good economic sense did not make good political sense. Maximizing behavior by politicians is seldom coincidental with the efficiency criteria of the economist. And the reason is not that the politician was typically making a trade-off between equity and efficiency. Usually the reason has more to do with the "realistic" constraints faced by the politician. It makes little sense to preach to politicians about what they should do. We need to understand what they can do. Economists and political scientists, belatedly, are beginning to explore those constraints.

(2) But exploring those constraints produces a quandary for economists. It is no accident that economic models of the polity as developed in the public choice literature make the State into something like the Mafia – or, to employ their terminology, a leviathan. The State was little more than a machine to redistribute wealth and income. These models had two essential neo-classical characteristics; one, they were devoid of institutions; and two, the political actors were wealth-maximizing politicians. The consequence was a state in which the distribution of "violence potential" dictated the relationship between rulers and constituents, and which was inherently unstable.[3]

We don't have to look very far afield to observe polities with these characteristics. But the traditional public choice literature is clearly not the whole story. Indeed it has misled us by failing to make us realize that successful economic growth necessitates the creation and enforcement by the State of economic rules that foster conditions conducive to such economic performance. But such a model involves not only institutions but significant modification of the behavioral assumptions that we economists employ. Let me elaborate first on the economic rules, then on the political rules, and then on the behavioral characteristics.

There is no great secret to the specification of property rights that broadly provide incentives for productive economic activity. As Professor Stiglitz pointed out, there is broad agreement as to their significance. The dilemma concerns their creation and enforcement. Take the characteristics of adaptive efficiency outlined above. Such a set of rules makes currently profitable and efficient enterprise less secure (thus the conflict between allocative and adaptive efficiency) by encouraging the creative destruction envisioned by Schumpeter. Not only do such rules encourage innovation and displacement, but they also wipe out losers. Now in that marvelous never-never land conjured up by welfare economists the gainers compensate the losers and all is well. But in our world they (for the most part) don't. And accordingly it is in the interests of existing firms, trade unions, farm groups, etc., to try to devise rules that protect their own (usually short-term) interests. Mancur Olson (1982) provides a portrait of the sclerotic consequences for economies that results from the long-run accumulation of such interest group pressures. But, unfortunately, he fails to provide any model of the polity that would give us insight into the political process that produces such adverse economic consequences.

That brings me to the political rules. Two centuries ago James Madison tried to devise a polity that avoided the problem of factions (groups pursuing their own interests at the expense of the rest of the populace), be they a majority or a minority. His solution was the system of checks and balances and the federal form of government embodied in the US Constitution. That document is still held up as the basic cause of US well-being and long-term success. But is it? Latin American countries imbued with the same ideas of liberty as their northern cousins became independent of Spain in the early nineteenth century and adopted US style constitutions; but they had radically different results. There is, then, more to institutions than formal rules. There are also the effectiveness of enforcement and norms of behavior – that is, informal constraints that supplement and modify formal rules.

The most distinguishing characteristic of the "successful" economies is their ability to realize the promise of modern technology and the consequent specialization and division of labor with contracts across time and space and with unknown second parties. Such contracts are a basic underlying requirement of efficient markets and necessitate effective third party enforcement. In turn that entails a polity and judicial system that impartially and rapidly adjudicates disputes with a consistent set of rules. While no society completely meets these requirements, developed countries come close enough to encourage such contracting. But how does a society achieve third party enforcement? Is there any way that a society of wealth-maximizing actors with diverse interests will construct and enforce a set of rules that will lead to a polity and judicial system with these essential features?

Norms of behavior entail informal constraints that can make formal rules more effective by altering discount rates or lowering information costs (see Milgrom, North, and Weingast, mimeo). They also entail self-imposed standards of conduct such as honesty and integrity which can effectively alter the costs of contracting in both the political (judicial) and economic realms. We don't always cheat, lie, and steal when we could get away with it. Judges are not always buyable, and politicians do frequently pay a big electoral price for their beliefs. Now it is true that "good institutions" effectively enforced can direct incentives towards productive activity. The plain fact is, however, that the costs of measurement and enforcement of contracts in the impersonal world of specialization that we have created offer ample opportunity for antisocial behavior; and without rules being supplemented by self-imposed standards of conduct which constrain maximization at some margins it is hard to believe that such complex societies would be viable.

But the economic models we employ have little room for such behavioral complexity. Trust, ethical standards of conduct, and moral precepts do influence the costs of contracting and the performance of economies, as also do ideologies such as communism and fundamentalist religious beliefs. A major challenge to the social scientist is to develop political-economic models that both are institutionally rich and can take into account more complex behavior than has been done heretofore. We may then be able to narrow the gap between what the role of the State should be and what it is feasible to expect of the State.

NOTES

1 For the story of this evolution, see North and Weingast (1988).
2 For a comparison of the Spanish and English experiences and the consequences for Latin America and North America respectively, see North (1988).
3 See Douglass North, "A neo-classical theory of the State," in North (1981) for an elaboration of this model.

REFERENCES

Alchian, A. (1950), "Uncertainty, evolution, and economic theory," *Journal of Political Economy*, 59.

Milgrom, Paul R., Douglass C. North, and Barry R. Weingast (1988), "Third party enforcement of norms and contracts: A theoretical and historical analysis," mimeo, Hoover Institution and Stanford University.

Nelson, Richard R. and Sidney G. Winter (1982), *An Evolutionary Theory of Economic Change* (Cambridge, MA: Belknap Press of Harvard University Press).

North, Douglass C. (1981), *Structure and Change in Economic History* (New York: W. W. Norton and Company).

North, Douglass C. (1988), "Institutions, economic growth, and freedom: an historical introduction," in M. Walker (ed.) *Freedom, Democracy, and Economic Welfare* (Vancouver: Fraser Institute).

North, Douglass C. and Barry R. Weingast (1988), "Constitutions and commitment: The evolution of institutions governing public choice in 17th century England," Working Paper, Hoover Institution.

Olson, Mancur (1982), *The Rise and Decline of Nations* (New Haven, CT: Yale University Press).

Schumpeter, Joseph A. (1954), "The crisis of the tax state," in A. Peacock, R. Turvey, W. F. Stolper, and E. Henderson (eds), *International Economic Papers*.

Comments 3

*Dieter Bös**

The Not-so-Universal, Not-so-Compulsory State	117
Normative Economic Theory	118
Positive Economic Theory	119
Open Economy	119
Fiscal Federalism	120
Incentive Compatibility	120
Shadow Economy	121
Stabilization, Distribution, and Allocation	122
The Neglect of Stabilization Problems	122
Redistribution of Real Incomes	123
Normative Approaches to Redistribution	123
Positive Approaches to Redistribution	125
Allocation	126
Policy Making and Economic Doctrines	128

THE NOT-SO-UNIVERSAL, NOT-SO-COMPULSORY STATE

According to Stiglitz, the main difference between the State and other economic organizations is as follows: only state membership is universal, only the State has the power of compulsion, in particular the power to tax (pp. 21–2). Stiglitz himself mentions some "caveats" (pp. 22–3), referring to voluntary compliance and minority interests. However, in the rest of his paper, in my opinion, he overstates the point of state compulsion.

Two hundred years after the French Revolution this seems to be a strange position. Over many centuries revolution and evolution have proved effective in changing state constitutions, the power to vote, the

---

* I gratefully acknowledge comments by Hans G. Helmstädter, Wolfgang Peters, Christian Scheer, and Friedrich Vogelbusch on the first draft of this paper.

power to tax, etc. In the long run, therefore, individuals matter more than any state compulsion. I personally hope that the recent developments in Eastern Europe will be one more proof of this general statement. One might come to the conclusion that states have full power of compulsion only if one ignored history.

However, even if we accept Stiglitz's non-historic view, I am not in full agreement with his view of the compulsory State. First, the extent of compulsion varies across states: in an Eastern European country a citizen may not actually have the right to exit. In Western European countries this right always exists. An Austrian citizen can leave Austria to work and live in Germany as easily as he can leave his firm and choose to work for another one. Second, state economic activities do not necessarily use the typical government authority. This is, of course, the case for legislation and administrative activities of a governmental nature. However, there are many administrative activities of a proprietary nature, as embedded in, for instance, public enterprises or public purchases. Here, the State behaves like any other economic agent. It does not use its compulsory power. If an employee wants to leave his position in a public enterprise, he is as free to do so as in a private enterprise. If somebody sells furniture to a government office, this is as much a contract as any other sale to non-government offices.[1]

Let us go one step further. Even if we exclude administrative activities of a proprietary nature, I am not in full agreement with Stiglitz's characterization of the State as a fully compulsory organization. In the following sections I shall illustrate why I believe his position is too strong.

Normative Economic Theory

Let me first begin with the long tradition of looking at the State as a voluntary organization. Such theories give interesting insights of a philosophical nature; however, I do not think they are an adequate description of economic reality of the various states we are facing in the twentieth century, either in the West or in the East. Since public economics deals not only with positive, but also with *normative approaches*,[2] it is appropriate that normative economics ponder over a conception of the State as a voluntary association. Such a treatment of the State includes not only Nozick's anarchy,[3] but Rawls's principles of equity;[4] and Brennan–Buchanan's[5] constitutional theories also start from a situation where the State is established out of the free will of all citizens. Isn't it appropriate for normative economics to consider which policy results if the government acts *as if* the State were a voluntary association? Isn't that the basis of economists postulating that the government should restrict its policy to Pareto-improving moves, which are unanimously accepted by all citizens? I do not argue that it is necessarily the best economic policy which results from such a position. Restricting economic policy to Pareto-improving moves will, in many cases, lead to situations which most people consider inequitable from the point of view of income distribution. However, in my opinion, it is an unnecessary restriction of normative economic theory to define the State only as a compulsory association.

Positive Economic Theory

For *positive economic theory* I agree it is not meaningful to describe the State as a completely voluntary association. However, it is too strong to say that the State is only a compulsory organization.[6] Recently, the limits to state compulsion have been accentuated in the literature of public economics. They were even overaccentuated by recent doctrines of the right. However, rejecting particular inadequacies of right-wing doctrines should not imply rejecting all limits to compulsion, as in Stiglitz's paper. Let us therefore give a short list of the most important limits to state compulsion. They all result from the citizens' reactions to state policies which must be taken into account by the government when setting the rules and actions of economic policy.

Open Economy

Citizens who dislike state policies are given the option to emigrate. For countries like the US or West Germany, it is mainly the other side of the coin which is of relevance: they attract people, thereby reducing the compulsion of other states. In Eastern Europe the compulsory nature of the State is higher than in Western Europe. By postulating that all states are compulsory organizations this difference is blurred. In Western Europe there is yet another important restriction on economic compulsion: in this area most states are members of the EC, which necessitates harmonization of economic policies and facilitates free mobility of labor and capital between states.

Fiscal Federalism[7]

If there is a three-tier system of states, there will be a system of checks and balances which reduces the compulsion of each and every government in this system. In many European states, federal laws have to pass not only the federal parliament, but also a second chamber, where representatives of the second tier of government decide upon acceptance or rejection of the act. In the first section of this paper I mentioned the obstacles to privatization which, in Germany, result from fiscal federalism. Similar restrictions of economic policy have occurred with respect to the recent reform of personal income taxation – and everybody knows the reform of business taxation will also run into difficulties caused by fiscal federalism. One of the most important German business taxes is a local tax which is imposed on the basis of a federal law (*Gewerbesteuer*). The abolition of this tax has been discussed for many years because (a) it implies a sort of double taxation of entrepreneurial activity – the business tax liability is added to the corporation income tax liability or to the personal income tax liability, and (b) it does not depend on the revenue of the firm and, therefore, also has to be paid in years of losses. At the basis of the local business tax is a federal law, therefore the tax can be abolished only by the federal government. However, as this tax is the backbone of local finance, the federal government would have to compensate the local communities.

Fiscal decentralization restricts governments' compulsion for yet another reason. The governments of the second and third tiers have to cope with the citizens voting with their feet: it is easier to move within one federal state than to go abroad, therefore citizens will do so if given some "rational" impetus. In this sense the compulsory power of local governments seems to be restricted to a higher extent than the compulsory power of the federal government.

Incentive Compatibility

The compulsory power of a state government is restricted by its lack of information. If the government were fully informed it could impose a system of lump-sum taxes to achieve a first-best optimum. Incomplete information leads to the problem of incentive compatibility. When the government plans an income tax, it assumes that the man with ability w_{115} earns an income y_{115}, which results from his individual utility-maximizing labor supply, adjusted to the income tax.[8] The tax must be designed in such a way that the government can be sure that the one who earns the income y_{115} must be the man with the ability w_{115}. This solves the problem of the government's not knowing who is who. If an income tax is not incentive compatible, it is possible that income y_{115} is earned by the man with ability w_{320}, say, who decided to "hide" his ability by earning a lower income than anticipated by the government. It is clear that the entire planning process of the government breaks down in such a case. The government had anticipated that the man with the ability w_{320} would earn income y_{320} and had planned its redistribution policy on the basis of this assumption.

However, this man has manipulated government policy. A consistent tax policy under incomplete information is possible only if the politician anticipates exactly how taxpayers would adjust and incorporates this adjustment in the tax policy. Then taxpayers actually behave as anticipated (revelation principle) and the plan of the politician is realized in practice. How can the government make sure that no one deviates from the behavior which was anticipated when the tax was designed? This can be guaranteed if each utility-maximizing individual attains his best result by "declaring" his ability or labor supply rather than by signaling false characteristics. To make sure the skilled participate in the economic system in a way which actually earns high incomes, the politician must consider the "self-selection" constraints of the taxpayers. Clearly these constraints restrict the feasible policies of the government.

It should be mentioned that Stiglitz is one of the pioneers of the above-mentioned approach. I am, therefore, surprised that he has not mentioned the extent to which state compulsion is restricted by citizens' ability to hide information.

Shadow Economy

State compulsion is also restricted by the impossibility of prosecuting all economic criminality. First this is an information problem: the government does not know of all economic crimes and it would be too costly to acquire such knowledge. This problem is not only a problem of Western economies, but is relevant also in Eastern Europe. Second, particular tax evasion may be possible because of the State's liberal self-commitments (where liberal is meant in the European sense).

STABILIZATION, DISTRIBUTION, AND ALLOCATION

The following treatment of the most important targets in public economics refers to all forms of government legislation and administration, including activities serving a proprietary function. Therefore, public enterprises, public purchases, and public subsidies are included in this analysis, as we are dealing with the economics of government behavior, not with the juridical problem of determining the extent of government sovereignty.

The Neglect of Stabilization Problems

If an author writes about the economic role of the State and intends to dismantle the value judgments of doctrines of the New Right, he must not omit the most important challenge of these doctrines, which consists of an attack on the Keynesian stabilization policies.[9] Monetarism has accentuated the crowding-out effects of government spending and the dominant role of monetary policy. The macroeconomics of monetarism can be characterized as a theory of inflation, not of employment or stability. Politicians are asked to refrain from discrete interventions, and to stick to rules: for instance, a steady rate of monetary growth.[10] More recently, the classic view that the private sector is inherently stable has been revived. Business cycles have been treated as equilibrium phenomena.[11] If a government announces a policy in order to reduce cyclical fluctuations, such a policy is futile because of rational expectations of the economic agents. All possible consequences of Keynesian policy are fully anticipated and hence counteracted by the individuals. If the government avoids an explicit announcement, the policy may be successful in the short run, but leads to long-run distortions due to increased uncertainty of private economic agents. Such a government loses its reputation.

In Stiglitz's paper the role of government in economic stabilization has not been considered.[12] Terms such as "rational expectations" or "reputation" of the government are not even mentioned in the paper.

Furthermore, it is doubtful that the private sector is as inherently stable as monetarism assumes. Rational expectations, in my opinion, are convenient in mathematical modeling, but are not a realistic description of economic agents. The super-rational individual, which is postulated in these models, simply does not exist. Such a view fits nicely into the main tendencies of Stiglitz's paper. Non-rational expectations constitute a sort of market failure. However, they lead to the possibility of successful stabilization policy. The stabilization policy, in turn, may exploit the non-rational expectations – for instance, when the economic agents forget relevant policy actions. So political business cycles might occur which constitute a sort of government failure.

It may be noted that stabilization problems are neglected in many recent books and papers in public economics. Musgrave's standard work[13] dealt with the issues of allocation, distribution, and stabilization; however, recently public economists have concentrated on allocation and distribution only. Stabilization has been relegated to macroeconomics. This could be regarded as convenient scientific labor-sharing. However, this labor-sharing runs the risk of losing the connections between the three most important goals of public economics!

Redistribution of Real Incomes

Normative Approaches to Redistribution

Let us first recall how Stiglitz treats the normative approaches to redistribution. On pp. 28–9 he argues that it is often unclear what is equitable and fair. In what follows normative problems are put aside, they reappear only in note 59, where Ramsey–Boiteux pricing is rejected, but optimal income taxation accepted.

The examples Stiglitz presents on pp. 28–9 show that government policies can be regarded as equitable or inequitable according to the chosen concept of equity (or fairness). Equity, as a difficult problem, has been given many different meanings both in theory and in practice. However, this does not mean that the concept of equity is futile. It is not even indeterminate. A rational politician who proposes some particular move in the interest of what he considers fair, is fully consistent in his behavior and follows one particular well-defined concept of equity. Some rational member of the opposition may disagree and claim the move is unfair, given some other definition of fairness, and this is also consistent behavior. Such discussions do not render redistribution meaningless. The politician who applies some particular concept of fairness should know a majority is backing him, otherwise the fairness concept proposed by the opposition might be decisive to his losing the next election.

In theory it is even easier to start from various definitions of equity and fairness and to compare the resulting fiscal policies. Stiglitz seems to believe normative redistribution concepts require one and only one definition of fairness. However, economists must accept there are many possible definitions of fairness which play a role in the political process. It is no counterargument to redistribution policy that "it is not always obvious what is fair." There are many principles to judge whether a situation is fair, and normative theory remains meaningful in showing the results which follow from accepting some particular principle. Moreover, dealing with the role of various definitions of fairness and incorporating these into models of competition between political parties is a fascinating exercise in normative modeling.

Cross-subsidization (pp. 52–3) is a special form of redistribution which has been opposed heavily. Stiglitz argues that public pricing, even including Ramsey–Boiteux pricing, should be restricted to allocation, whereas income redistribution remains the domain of subsidization and income taxation. His main argument is informational in nature and I do not believe it. Basically he argues that the demand functions for publicly provided goods cannot be estimated empirically: "the information required for its implementation is in general not available." I disagree: demand functions can be estimated.[14] Determining Ramsey–Boiteux prices is no more complicated than determining monopolistic prices; in fact, they have the same price structure. Stiglitz's criticism becomes even stranger when he says: "in fact, in the presence of an (optimal) income tax, uniform mark-ups may in fact be optimal." This implies, according to Stiglitz, that Ramsey–Boiteux prices demand too much information, whereas an optimal income tax does not require as much information. I disagree. The computation of the optimal income tax requires at least as much information as the computation of Ramsey–Boiteux prices.[15]

Positive Approaches to Redistribution

When dealing with positive approaches to redistribution, Stiglitz begins with destructive criticism. Redistribution is traced back to the rent-seeking activity of interest groups. Redistribution is a sort of public hypocrisy (p. 29). Politicians often consider "the appearance of equity" as "more important than the reality" (p. 29). Even worse, "the equity constraint results in government programs that are ill-suited to any 'rational' objective" (p. 61). After learning that redistribution means hypocrisy and is irrational, the reader is suddenly confronted with a complete U-turn on p. 61: "The fact that, in ... redistributing income, some income gets redistributed to the well-off, ... does not necessarily mean that the government programs should be eliminated. It only means that there is an added 'cost' to the program which needs to be taken into account in judging whether it is worthwhile."

To put it mildly, Stiglitz's presentation is misleading. Obviously, in his opinion there are two kinds of redistribution policies: desired and not-desired ones. Putting all redistributions out into the open should result in retaining the desired activities and abolishing the not-desired policies. This point of view *first* requires some yardstick which allows us to distinguish between desired and not-desired activities. In my opinion, it is here that we must return to the normative approach of equity and fairness. Politicians and voters must make particular judgments as to what is fair. The theorist then can offer precise formulations of various concepts and voters may choose from any of them. *Second*, we should face the fact that both desirable and non-desirable redistribution may result from rent-seeking. It is misleading to condemn all activities of interest groups. If an interest group looks after the well-being of elderly retired people and succeeds in persuading a politician to pass some special law in favor of the very poor retired portion of the population, we should welcome this activity. The same holds for particular interest groups who act in the interest of less developed countries.

However, I fully agree with Stiglitz's claim for bringing redistributions "out into the open." A good example are interest groups which act in favor of less developed countries. As we all know, this is an area both of desirable and non-desirable redistributions.

Allocation[16]

Recently, I have written a number of papers on the privatization of public enterprises. Here the allocational problems are of particular importance and some of the arguments of Stiglitz's essay can be supported by referring to my earlier studies.

Many empirical studies confirm that private enterprises typically are more efficient than public enterprises which operate in a comparable environment.[17] The X-inefficient behavior of public firms, however, is very difficult to treat in neo-classical modeling. Here we tend to think along neo-classical lines. Movements which happen below these lines sometimes follow unexpected criteria. For example, it is well known[18] that sometimes it may be welfare-improving to increase the inefficiency of production. Moreover, we do not know precisely which incentives matter within the inefficient space unless we choose some functional description of the behavior of inefficient agents within the inefficient space. However, such theories very often require assumptions which are rather ad hoc.

Two typical examples are the following. When a public enterprise is privatized, the government will want to predict how the efficiency of the firm changes if the extent of privatization increases. Such a prediction requires a production function which is shifted according to the extent of privatization,[19] until it is either impossible to increase efficiency by further increasing the extent of privatization, or until 100 percent of the firm has been sold to private owners. This is an attempt to model the behavior within the space of inefficient input–output combinations. A similar procedure has been applied by Gravelle,[20] who postulates a production function which is shifted depending on higher or lower effort of the managers.

In another attempt to model the behavior of a public firm in the inefficient space, I assume that trade unions are responsible for inefficiency.[21] The production function relates the one output of the model to the capital input and the optimal amount of labor which is necessary for any combination of capital and output. In this model, trade unions have an objective function which depends on wages and on some inefficient over-employment.[22] In the firm, representatives of trade unions and the firm's managers compromise over the actual number of persons employed. Hence this is also an ad hoc theory to model the inefficient behavior of the firm.

The ideas of the preceding paragraphs lead us directly to the next problem. It is not only the incentives within the firm which are still insufficiently modeled from a more advanced theoretical point of view. If we explicitly try to consider the principal–agent relation between the firm and some regulating authority, it is the lack of information which becomes of decisive importance. I shall not deal with that problem too intensively.[23] I only want to stress that the principal–agent approaches of the public firm face problems similar to the modeling of inefficiency mentioned above. Consider, for instance, Baron and Myerson's[24] approach of regulating a firm under unknown costs. The cost function of that model is shifted according to a parameter which is exactly known only to the firm, and the government is incompletely informed. It knows only the distribution function of that parameter. We have a specified cost function where some additional parameter is introduced ad hoc to cope with the problems of information and incentive structures. Therefore we find the same basic modeling problem in these approaches to regulation that are evident in my models on privatization and (in other papers) on public enterprise economics which try to deal explicitly with the incentives of managers within some inefficient space of input–output combinations.

Modeling the incentives of the firm, given imperfect information in the government or some other regulating authority, has become one of the main concerns in the recent theory of public and regulated private enterprises.[25] This recent theory implies that it is not ownership as such which makes the difference between a public firm and a regulated private firm. Ownership matters for the distribution of income and wealth; however, these distributions are only in the background of theoretical modeling. In the foreground of recent theories we find a discussion of incentives and the particular distribution of information which result from the distribution of ownership and from regulatory constraints. It is this difference in incentives and information, not in ownership, which constitutes the difference between public firms and regulated private firms according to the state of the art. I admit, however, that I am always puzzled by this position of recent economic theory.

POLICY MAKING AND ECONOMIC DOCTRINES

The intentions of Stiglitz's paper on the economic role of the State are clear. They are stated on p. 57: "Socialism as an economic doctrine ... is now dead. What I fear, however, is that the inadequacies of the doctrines of the right will only gradually become apparent." For a US economist this may be an interesting insight. For most European countries, in my opinion, the statement on socialism is wrong and the statement on the New Right is unnecessary, because this doctrine is not relevant in most parts of Europe. The eclectic position Stiglitz is advocating has been applied in Germany for at least the past 15 years. My rejection of Stiglitz's argument may be substantiated by means of two examples: the recent German policies on privatization and on tax reform.

What is called "privatization" in Germany is very different from recent privatization in the UK and in France.[26] When the German federal government speaks of privatization, it means, for instance, selling the remaining 16 percent of its shares in the Volkswagenwerk. The government does not even think of selling vital public utilities, but intends only to reorganize the public enterprise, such as that which produces postal and telecommunication services. The present strength of German trade unions, which are adamantly opposed to privatization and exert a strong influence on political parties, is a major impediment to any privatization in West Germany.[27] The German trade unions' opposition to privatization results mainly from the fear of employees in public firms that they will lose their privileges. Public firms' employees may have to face wage reductions in the event of privatization.[28] Even worse problems would arise in industries such as mail and rail (*Bundespost* and *Bundesbahn*), where many employees have civil servant status.[29] Moreover, many public enterprises are owned by states (*Länder*) and by local communities. Needless to say, social democratic governments or social democratic mayors of large cities have no intention of privatizing.

In a similar way, what is called "tax reform" in Germany is very different from recent tax reforms in the US and in the UK.[30] The reform of the income tax schedule retained the 53 percent marginal tax rate for the highest income earners, which is high in terms of relative standards. The choice of a linearly increasing marginal tax rate admittedly reduces the tax pressure in the medium income areas. However, it is not based on any explicit theory of the disincentive effects of income taxation. It was the a priori intention of German politicians that the marginal tax rate *must* increase with increasing income, up to a maximum of 53 percent. Furthermore, German politicians still believe in traditional social democratic fine-tuning by tax exemptions. At least there are so many exemptions left that one hesitates to speak of a tendency towards a comprehensive income tax.

NOTES

1 There can be an asymmetric distribution of power if the government is a monopolistic buyer. However, this is a problem of economic power, not a juridical problem of compulsion: nobody can be obliged juridically to sell to the State, although his economic position may compel him to do so.
2 And Stiglitz (p. 12) explicitly emphasizes that he wants to deal with *both* approaches.
3 Nozick (1974).
4 Rawls (1972).
5 Brennan and Buchanan (1980, 1986).
6 Moreover, it is too strong to say that *only* the State is a compulsory organization. There is a whole spectrum of intermediate forms from completely voluntary to completely compulsory organizations. Good examples are social insurance institutions and trade unions in many European countries.
7 This problem is treated in Stiglitz, pp. 45ff, but not from the point of view of possible restrictions on government compulsion.
8 We exclude bunching of incomes.
9 There exists serious criticism which is put forward within the Keynesian IS–LM approach. By adding a government budget constraint to the usual IS–LM model, and by explicitly allowing for wealth effects and interest payments, some theorists proved the possible instability of debt-financed government spending. See Blinder and Solow (1973) and Turnovsky (1977), pp. 79–85.
10 See Friedman (1969).
11 See, for instance, the overviews in Barro (1981) and Lucas and Sargent (1981).

12 See p. 13 and the note 67 of the paper.
13 Musgrave (1959).
14 As only one example I may be allowed to mention my own estimation of Ramsey–Boiteux prices for London Transport. See Bös (1986a), pp.317–423.
15 For a more extensive discussion of the combination of optimal income taxation and public sector pricing, see Bös (1984).
16 This subsection relies heavily on Bös (1988c).
17 For good surveys see Borcherding, Pommerehne and Schneider (1982), Millward (1982), and Millward and Parker (1983).
18 See Smith (1983) and Peters (1985).
19 See Bös (1986b, 1987, 1988a) and Bös and Peters (1988).
20 See Gravelle (1982).
21 See Bös (1988b).
22 This seems to be a good description of Austrian and British trade unions' behavior until recently.
23 For a recent survey see Guesnerie (1988).
24 See Baron and Myerson (1982).
25 For instance Vickers and Yarrow (1988), pp. 35–9, 91–101, and Rees (1988).
26 See Bös (1989a).
27 Von Loesch (1983) and Vogelsang (1988).
28 Windisch (1987), p. 23.
29 Vogelsang (1988).
30 See Bös (1989b).

REFERENCES

Baron, D. P. and R. B. Myerson (1982), "Regulating a monopolist with unknown costs," *Econometrica*, 50, pp. 911–30.

Barro, R. (1981), "The equilibrium approach to business cycles," in R. Barro (ed.), *Money Expectations and Business Cycles* (New York: Academic Press).

Blinder, A. and R. Solow (1973), "Does fiscal policy matter?," *Journal of Public Economics*, 2, pp. 319–37.

Bös, D. (1984), "Income taxation, public sector pricing and redistribution," *Scandinavian Journal of Economics*, 86, pp. 166–83.

Bös, D. (1986a), *Public Enterprise Economics* (Amsterdam: North-Holland).
Bös, D. (1986b), "A theory of the privatization of public enterprises," in D. Bös and C. Seidl (eds), *Welfare Economics of the Second Best, Journal of Economics/Zeitschrift für Nationalökonomie*, Supplement 5, (Vienna: Springer).
Bös, D. (1987), "Privatization of public enterprises," *European Economic Review*, 31, pp. 352–60.
Bös, D. (1988a), "Welfare effects of privatizing public enterprises," in D. Bös, M. Rose, and C. Seidl (eds), *Welfare and Efficiency in Public Economics* (Berlin, Heidelberg, and New York: Springer), pp. 339–62.
Bös, D. (1988b), "Privatization of public firms: A government–trade union–private shareholder cooperative game," in M. Neumann (ed.), *Public Finance and the Performance of Enterprises* (Detroit, MI: Wayne State University Press, forthcoming).
Bös, D. (1988c), "Recent theories in public enterprise economics," *European Economic Review*, 32, pp. 409–14.
Bös, D. (1989a), "Arguments on privatization," in W. Fels and G. von Fürstenberg (eds), *A Supply Side Agenda for Germany* (Heidelberg and Berlin: Springer).
Bös, D. (1989b), "Tax reform in Germany," mimeo, Bonn.
Bös, D. and W. Peters (1988), "Privatization, efficiency, and market structure," in B. Rudolph and J. Wilhelm (eds), *Bankpolitik, finanzielle Unternehmensführung und die Theorie der Finanzmärkte* (Berlin: Duncker & Humblot), pp. 367–92.
Borcherding, T. E., W. W. Pommerehne and F. Schneider (1982), "Comparing the efficiency of private and public production: The evidence from five countries," in D. Bös, R. A. Musgrave, and J. Wiseman (eds), *Public Production, Journal of Economics/Zeitschrift für Nationalökonomie*, Supplement 2 (Vienna: Springer).
Brennan, G. and J. Buchanan (1980), *The Power to Tax* (Cambridge: Cambridge University Press).
Brennan, G. and J. Buchanan (1986), *The Reason of Rules* (Cambridge: Cambridge University Press).
Friedman, M. (1969), "The role of monetary politics," *The Optimum Quantity of Money and Other Essays* (Chicago: Aldine).
Gravelle, H. S. E. (1982), "Incentives, efficiency and control in public firms," in D. Bös, R. A. Musgrave, and J. Wiseman (eds),

Public Production, *Journal of Economics/Zeitschrift für Nationalökonomie*, Supplement 2 (Vienna: Springer).

Guesnerie, R. (1988), "Regulation as an adverse selection problem," *European Economic Review*, 32, pp. 473–81.

Heald, D. (1989), "The United Kingdom: Privatisation and its political context," *Western European Politics*, vol. 11, no. 4 (forthcoming).

Loesch, A. von (1983), *Privatisierung öffentlicher Unternehmen: Ein Überblick über die Argumente, Schriftenreihe der Gesellschaft für öffentliche Wirtschaft und Gemeinwirtschaft*, no. 23 (Baden-Baden: Nomos Verlagsgesellschaft).

Lucas, R. and T. Sargent (1981), *Rational Expectations and Econometric Practice* (Minneapolis: Allen & Unwin).

Millward, R. (1982), "The Comparative Performance of Public and Private Ownership," in Lord Roll, *The Mixed Economy* (London: Macmillan; New York: Holmes and Meier); reprinted in J. A. Kay, C. P. Mayer, and D. J. Thompson (eds), *Privatisation and Regulation: The UK experience* (Oxford: Clarendon Press, 1986).

Millward, R. and D. M. Parker (1983), "Public and private enterprise: Comparative behaviour and relative efficiency," in R. Millward, D. Parker, L. Rosenthal, M. T. Sumner, and N. Topham (eds), *Public Sector Economics* (London: Longman).

Musgrave, R. A. (1959), *The Theory of Public Finance* (New York: McGraw-Hill).

R.Nozick (1974), *Anarchy, State, and Utopia* (Oxford: Basil Blackwell).

Peters, W. (1985), "Can inefficient public production promote welfare?," *Journal of Economics/Zeitschrift für Nationalökonomie*, 45, pp. 395–407.

Rawls, J. (1972), *A Theory of Justice* (Oxford: Clarendon Press).

Rees, R. (1988), "Privatisation, investment and risk," *European Economic Review*, 32, pp. 422–31.

Smith, A. (1983), "Tax reform and temporary inefficiency," *Journal of Public Economics*, 20, pp. 265–70.

Turnovsky, S. J. (1977), *Macroeconomic Analysis and Stabilization Policy* (Cambridge: Cambridge University Press).

Vickers, J. and G. Yarrow (1988), *Privatization* (Cambridge, MA: MIT Press).

Vogelsang, I. (1988), "Deregulation and privatization in the Federal Republic of Germany," mimeo, Rand Corporation WD–3837–MF.

Windisch, R. (1987), "Privatisierung natürlicher Monopole: Theoretische Grundlagen und Kriterien," in R. Windisch (ed.), *Privatisierung natürlicher Monopole im Bereich von Bahn, Post und Telekommunikation* (Tübingen: Mohr).

Comments 4

Chris Freeman

The paper by Professor Stiglitz is a very useful and balanced assessment of a debate which has rumbled on for more than two centuries and has become particularly intense in the most recent period. The debate is certainly not over yet. His argument that privatization is not necessarily better "but that the process of change will have beneficial effects" in itself (p. 56) is, as he points out in relation to Hirschman, a two-edged argument. His overall view appears to be that the tide of privatization has now turned and that at least in the US, if not yet in Europe, there is a renewed recognition of some functions which are often better performed by the State and some disenchantment with "deregulation" (p. 20).

An interesting question is whether this swing of fashionable economic doctrine and the related swings of public opinion (favoring more or less regulation or intervention) are of long or short duration. Only an historical approach can satisfactorily address this question.

Clearly there is insufficient space to do more than touch on some of the fundamental problems. A fuller development of the theme may be found in the book edited by Dosi, Freeman, Nelson, Silverberg, and Soete (1988) and in particular in the chapter by Freeman and Perez. Like the original Stiglitz paper, this comment will not deal with the experience of the communist countries, despite its relevance.

One justification for an historical rather than a purely theoretical approach to the problem lies in the obvious fact that the changing structure of all industrialized economies (and of developing countries, too, for that matter) leads to a constant redefinition of the problem. An obvious case in point is the shift from atomistic small firm competition in the early nineteenth century to the giant firms and oligopolistic competition of the early twentieth century. Another is the rise of entirely new technologies, such as electric power, telecommunications, or electronic computers. Finally, the changing nature of environmental hazards, from the Alkali Acts of the 1860s to the disposal of nuclear waste and the "greenhouse" problems of the

1980s, serves again to emphasize the changing nature of the State's role and the increasingly international dimension of the problem.

Another justification for an historical approach rather than a neo-classical or welfare economics approach lies in the limitations of those theories themselves. It is increasingly recognized, both within the paradigm and outside it, that an "optimal" allocation of resources is a path-dependent historical process (Hahn, 1987). The notion that there is some kind of "absolute" optimum which can be determined by pure theory and defined as the closest possible approximation to perfect competition under all historic circumstances must be regarded as an ideological Utopia rather than a scientific endeavor or a practical possibility. The uncertainties involved in technical and social change are such that the rational, optimizing, calculating, and all-knowing behavior postulated as characteristic of entrepreneurs and other economic agents cannot be supported by empirical observations in any of the social sciences. Nor can the fundamental shortcomings of the theory be salvaged by the "as if" assumptions of "rational expectations" theory (Winter, 1986). The State certainly cannot be perfectly informed and wise in its allocation of resources: neither can the private market mechanism, particularly in relation to the long-term consequences of investment decisions involving technical change.

Consequently, the division of functions between states and private agents must be regarded less as the result of the rational triumph of pure economic theory and more as the outcome of an historical process involving complex social learning phenomena of individual agents and groups and the associated social and political conflicts. Stiglitz is refreshingly realistic about this, as when he points to the ideological bias and the inconsistencies in many preconceptions and popular attitudes. Sometimes, however, he appears to assume, at least implicitly, some superior wisdom in the competitive market mechanism, for example in his discussion of the "control and planning fallacies" (pp. 33–6). But he is very well aware that the forms of competition necessary to satisfy the ideal requirements of a rigorous theory are seldom if ever present, and his general approach is non-ideological and pragmatic. It is fairly obvious that no industrialized economic system could operate at all without some coordinating and regulatory activity by the State and that the forms of this activity must surely vary over time (Polanyi, 1944).

Thus, one way of looking at the debate over the last two centuries or so is in terms of a "trial and error" process of defining and redefining the boundaries of private enterprise and public intervention and the forms of that interrelation. There are obviously enormous variations between countries over time and many temporary reversals of the main trend, but we may distinguish two periods when the tide was clearly flowing in one direction: (1) from 1776 to the 1870s, and (2) from the 1870s to the 1970s.

The coincidence of the publication of *The Wealth of Nations* and the American Declaration of Independence provides a convenient starting date for the first period in 1776. From that time onwards the general tendency of economic and trade policy for about a century could be described as broadly in the direction of "laisser-faire" and free trade. Lassalle's "night-watchman state" always had, of course, other regulatory functions in addition to the protection of property and the enforcement of contracts. Proposals for new forms of intervention became increasingly frequent in the nineteenth century, as for example with the social legislation in Britain in the 1840s or Peel's Banking Act of 1844, but the broad tendency favored minimal functions for the State.

The appeal to the self-interest of the rising bourgeoisie was probably the major factor in the success of classical economic theory in redrawing the boundaries of state intervention in the general direction of laisser-faire. Smith's demonstration that, by pursuing their own goals of private accumulation of wealth, the entrepreneurs were also enhancing the public good was an extremely convenient rationalization and one which has shown far greater resilience than the corollary of effective price competition. The idea of a happy coincidence between private greed and public benefit was not, of course, original to classical economic theory. It was the central theme of Mandeville's *Fable of the Bees* in 1714. Mandeville not only developed the notion of "private vices and public virtue" but also of the division of labor and exchange. Adam Smith clothed these embryonic propositions with the force of a scientific truth with his theorems on specialization, scale economies, trade, size of markets, and price competition. The "invisible hand" served the dual function of a pure theory of economics and a moral sanction for laisser-faire capitalism.

In sweeping away the medieval and neo-mercantilist forms of regulation of production and trade, the arguments of Adam Smith and the classical economists appeared irrefutable and carried all before them in the late eighteenth and early nineteenth centuries. Margaret Thatcher was certainly not the first Prime Minister to offer genuflections to an economist guru. It was William Pitt who said to Adam Smith: "We are all your pupils now." However, the pragmatic demonstration of England's (and Scotland's) successful industrialization and technological achievements was at least as important as the theoretical arguments of Smith, Ricardo, and Mill, cogent and elegant though they were. The judgment of public opinion and posterity was formed on the basis of the performance of Britain in delivering growth and prosperity over the long term.

Moreover, there was a subtle difference between the laisser-faire message as interpreted in the leading industrial country – Britain – and the revisionist message propagated in the "latecomer" or newly industrializing countries of the nineteenth century. Most notably in Germany in the work of Friedrich List, but to a lesser degree in many other countries, the message was significantly diluted by a much stronger emphasis on the economic role of the State in its capacity as coordinator of the catching-up process. Both the goals of economic policy and the information needed to attain them are far more easily defined by the State in a catching-up situation.

By the 1870s and 1880s it was clear that the tide was turning away from laisser-faire and not only in the "catching-up" countries but also in Britain, the citadel of classical economics. The shift is foreshadowed by a comparison of the works of James Mill with the autobiography of his son John Stuart Mill (1873). In his later work, John Stuart Mill went so far as to call himself a "socialist," mainly on the grounds of the need for state redistributive policies and other types of reforming social legislation. By the 1880s a Liberal politician could say: "We are all socialists now," not, of course, in the Marxist sense, but in the sense of accepting that in many areas of economic activity there was a clear case for an increased degree of state involvement and regulation. In much the same vein Keynes could speak half a century later of the need for the "socialisation of investment." In both cases the depressed state of the economy heightened the pressures for more active state policies.

As the nineteenth century moved to its end the range of state involvement in the economy had been greatly enlarged, although it was still minute compared with the developments which followed in the twentieth century. Among the areas of increased involvement in the 1880s and 1890s were pensions and insurance, pollution prevention and abatement, public ownership of "utilities" or "natural monopolies," regulation of communications, tariffs and quotas, agricultural cooperatives and support schemes, regulation of banking and credit, and public health. Exceptions to "laisser-faire" proliferated and found their doctrinal sanction in various qualifications to competition theory.

However, perhaps the most interesting enlargement of the economic role of the State was in the area of education, training, science, and technology. In his concern to show how Germany might catch up with Britain, Friedrich List (1841) had pointed to the British technological lead as the crucial problem. He did not believe that the self-adjusting market mechanism would generate a catching-up process. On the contrary, he believed that free trade and competition between countries of great disparity in technological capacity would disadvantage the latecomers through the cumulative effects of what we would now call static and dynamic economies of scale. He therefore advocated an active state policy of industrialization and technology transfer with a very strong emphasis on skill formation through the state promotion of education and training and the import of skilled craftsmen from Britain.

Following the unification of the German states under Prussian leadership by 1871, it proved possible for the new Imperial German State to pursue the goals of economic nationalism prescribed by List with a high degree of success. The basic shift in technology from steam power to electric power and the new processes in steel production gave great advantages to large-scale producers capable of applying the new techniques in a more systematic way. The German electrical, chemical, and steel firms now rapidly overtook their British competitors. But this would hardly have been possible had they not enjoyed the advantage of a supply of skilled graduate engineers and technicians from the new "Technische Hochschulen" and from the expanding science faculties and postgraduate research activities of German universities. Less obvious but equally important for high technical standards and rapid technical advance was the establishment of the state "Physikalische und Technische Reichsanstalt" in the 1880s, and the Kaiser Wilhelm Institutes which followed it.

In other European countries and, of course, in the US more than anywhere else, a combination of public policies and private initiatives built up a system of higher education whose scope far surpassed that of Britain. Neither market forces nor state initiatives proved capable of reversing the long-term relative decline in the quality and skills of the British labor force and management for more than half a century. To this day the skill composition of the labor force remains a matter of deep concern (Prais, 1987) and in the view of many economists has been a major contributory factor to the relatively poor productivity performance of the British economy over a long period.

Evidently, therefore, the economic role of the State in relation to education and research must be recognized as of major importance, since the capacity to introduce and exploit new technologies efficiently now depends entirely on these activities. In its turn the long-term growth of any economy depends on this capability. It was not, therefore, surprising that in addition to many other areas of increased public expenditure and involvement the commitment to education, training, and research increased by orders of magnitude in the twentieth century in many countries.

The role of the State in relation to education, training, research, and technology must surely be included in a satisfactory discussion of the economic role of the State, and not only because of the particular case of Imperial Germany. It is widely recognized in neo-classical theory that there is a powerful argument for state involvement in these areas for a variety of reasons. The extraordinarily rapid growth of public education and R & D expenditures in the twentieth century must be attributed in part to this recognition, but in part also to the success of the German "model" and of a comparable expansion of public education and later of basic research in the US and other countries. This was an international "learning" process based on the comparative performance of various national economies and national systems of innovation. It is a process which strongly influenced Japanese state policies following the Meiji restoration in 1868. Indeed it can be argued that the "invisible hand" of the Japanese state in coordinating the Japanese efforts in technology and education has been the most successful example of the economic role of the State in the twentieth century (Freeman, 1987). It may prove even more important in the twenty-first century as the Japanese model is emulated in Korea and other countries.

Stiglitz necessarily had to confine his attention to certain areas of economic activity, but any comprehensive discussion of the economic role of the State must also surely emphasize its role in relation to the currency and the business cycle. After World War II there was a widespread public belief, reinforced by the Keynesian "revolution" in economic theory, that various forms of "market failure" were responsible for the Great Depression of the 1930s. The great extensions of public ownership, neo-Keynesian fiscal policies, and a vast increase in a wide variety of forms of state intervention which characterized the postwar period up to the 1970s can only be understood in this historical context. The Keynesian postwar welfare state was the culmination of a long period of increased state involvement, based on disillusion with private market forces.

One major difficulty in attempting to isolate the "economic" role of the State from its political, social, and military role is that its various functions are closely interdependent. This led Hayek (1944) and many other liberal economists to argue that an extension of state ownership or other forms of state involvement in the economy necessarily led to a totalitarian repressive political system. On the whole, experience did not support his view. Western European countries with a large public sector did not become totalitarian countries except when temporarily occupied by Nazi Germany. The Hitler régime, although vastly enlarging the German state by rearmament, repression, and military expansion, left most of the economy in private hands. Since World War II many countries have increased the economic role of the State while becoming more liberal and democratic in their political régimes.

The 1980s swing to economic liberalism and the attempts to "roll back" the frontier of state ownership and involvement in the economy must therefore be attributed more to the perceived failures of state economic activity than to a political protest against the power of the State. The inflationary pressures of the 1970s, the slowdown in the growth of the world economy, the apparent inefficiency and loss-making of some state enterprises all contributed to a climate of public opinion favoring a reduction in the economic role of the State. How should this 1980s swing be interpreted? Was it a temporary blip in a continuing long-term trend towards an increased economic role for the State? Or did it mark a major reversal of that trend leading to a long period of diminished state involvement?

These brief comments have suggested that the acceptance or rejection of specific economic functions of the State have depended on the one hand on the perceived performance of different types of economy and different types of state intervention over long periods of growth or stagnation, and on the other hand on "fire brigade" types of intervention to deal with particular emergencies, such as depressions. Until the 1870s, the régimes of regulation which were established involved minimal state involvement. But after the depressions of the 1870s to the 1890s, and even more after the depression of the 1930s, the regulation régimes became both far more expansive and far more comprehensive.

The paper by Stiglitz provides a useful guide as to which types of intervention are most likely to survive the present phase of "deregulation" and roll-back of the frontiers of state activity.

What *has* significantly diminished and is likely to continue to do so is the direct state operation of industries and services for the kind of reasons identified by Stiglitz. In some cases this may involve a direct return to private ownership by flotation in the capital market; in others a management buy-out; in others various forms of cooperative ownership; and in still others decentralized and devolved forms of public ownership. The parallel movement of devolution and decentralization of management responsibilities in the socialist countries suggests that this is indeed a strong and persistent worldwide trend.

However, this type of devolution and greater reliance on market mechanisms in many areas of the economy does not necessarily mean that a general long-term trend towards early nineteenth-century levels of state involvement is either probable or desirable. Those who imagine it is likely might reflect on why it was that the quarter century after World War II was a "golden age" of growth and prosperity throughout the world economy, yet it was also the period of maximum state involvement and regulation at the national and international levels. The qualifications which have been made above must be taken into account. These qualifications are: first, the historical experience of international competition and business cycles has demonstrated the increased importance of the State's involvement in education and research. Secondly, it has demonstrated the inevitable involvement of the State in attempting to cope with the problems of currency instability, international exchange rates, interest rates, and confidence in the banking and credit system. Finally, it is clear that the new technologies (biotechnology, computer networks, data banks, cheap universal international telecommunications, space technology) have already brought with them new requirements for regulation and deregulation. It is a commonplace that there has never been so much regulation of telecommunications systems as in the present phase of "deregulation." If we add to this the long-term global environmental hazards posed by nuclear power, acid rain, heavy metals, the greenhouse effect, etc., then it is a fairly safe bet that the regulatory and coordinating role of the State and of the international community is unlikely to diminish significantly. But the nature and forms of such involvement are sure to go on changing.

REFERENCES

Dosi, G., C. Freeman, R. Nelson, G. Silverberg, and L. Soete (eds) (1988), *Technical Change and Economic Theory* (London: Pinter; New York: Columbia UP).

Freeman, C. (1987), *Technology Policy and Economic Performance: Lessons from Japan* (London: Pinter).

Hahn, F. (1987), "Information dynamics and equilibrium," *Scottish Journal of Political Economy*.

Hayek, F. A. von (1944), *The Road to Serfdom* (Chicago: University of Chicago Press).

List, F. (1841), *The National System of Political Economy*, English translation (London: Dent).

Mill, J. S. (1873), *An Autobiography* (London: Longmans, Green, Reader, and Dyer).

Polanyi, K. (1944), *The Great Transformation* (New York: Reinhart).

Prais, S. (1987), "Educating for productivity," *National Institute Economic Review*, no. 119, pp. 40–56.

Winter, S. G. (1986), "Adoptive behaviour and economic rationality: Comments on Arrow and Lucas," *Journal of Business*, 59, pp. 427–34.

Comments 5

A. H. E. M. Wellink*

Introduction	145
An Ever-recurring Discussion	145
Balanced Assessment rather than Polarization	147
The Government as an Organization	149
The Government's Powers of Compulsion	149
Limits to the Government's Freedom to Act	149
Breach of Contract	150
Limits to Power in Specific Areas	152
Market Failure and Government Intervention	152
The Need for Government Intervention	153
Conflicting Aims of Government Intervention	153
The Form of Intervention	154
Delimitation of Tasks	155
Public Failure	156
Lack of Criteria for Action	156
Pressure Groups and the Influence of the Civil Service	157
Safeguards against Abuse of Power	158
Improving Government Efficacy and Efficiency	158
Privatization	159
Territorial Decentralization	161
An Outline of the Role of the Dutch Government in the 1990s	162

INTRODUCTION

An Ever-recurring Discussion

The role of the government in the economy was the subject of debate long before economics evolved into an independent science. As early as in the Greek era, this role was pondered by such philosophers as Socrates and Plato. At times, the debate subsides, only to flare up

* The author owes a deep debt of gratitude to H. J. Woltjer for his contribution to this article.

later with unexpected vehemence. Somewhat stylized, it may be observed that opinions move between the views of Adam Smith and those of Alexander Hamilton: at one extreme, the conviction that the government should refrain from intervention as the invisible hand of the price mechanism ensures adequate control and, at the other extreme, the belief that the State should intervene actively because the free play of market forces provides no adequate guarantee of a satisfactory (industrial) development.

In the debate on the role of the government, clearly oscillating movements have also been discernible in recent decades. In the 1960s and the early 1970s, internationally but in the Netherlands as well, the New Left highlighted the failure of the market and the government was assigned pride of place in the economic order. In Europe, in particular, the intellectual élite was strongly influenced by such left-wing philosophers as Sartre and Marcuse. Interest in a different, notably leftist, concept was fueled by opposition to the Vietnam War, and it was not only the US but the whole Western capitalist system of production which found itself in the dock. This process was boosted further by the wave of democratization originating from the student revolts. Additionally, the heavy emphasis which the post-Keynesian literature placed on the demand side of the economy and its focus on alternating over- and underproduction in the market sector bolstered the view that the government was to provide a counterweight and that its budgetary policy constituted an important controlling instrument. Galbraith's *The Affluent Society*, which fell on fertile ground in Dutch socialist circles in particular, inspired a strongly felt notion of insufficient public goods and services in a world flooded with market goods. Whether or not it was the normal disillusion which follows on an overaccentuation of the possibilities open to government, as Hirschman suggests (*Shifting Investments: Private interest and public action*, Princeton University Press, 1982), the ideas of the New Right gained the upper hand in the 1980s and, largely under the influence of monetarists such as Friedman and neo-classical economists such as Lucas, Sargent, and Wallace, the government's failure was highlighted and the market mechanism was restored to its position as the cornerstone of the economy.

A decisive element underlying the sharp revival of interest in the period 1980–2 in positive adjustment (supply-side policies or, formulated more broadly, widening the scope for the market and de-emphasizing the role of the government) has been the attitude of the major countries, initially notably the US (Reagan) and the UK (Thatcher). In these countries, ideological considerations played a large part in reducing government intervention. In the Netherlands, this process was set in motion for more pragmatic reasons and, hence, was more gradual and less polarizing. It was observed that the heavy burden of taxes and social insurance contributions had caused unduly high unemployment and it was concluded that the (relative) size of the public sector would have to be reduced. This does not, incidentally, mean that in the Netherlands ideological considerations are not playing any part whatever in the quest to come to a gradual reduction in government influence.

Balanced Assessment rather than Polarization

As Stiglitz rightly notes in his essay, it is important to avoid thinking in black-and-white terms, with the doctrinaire left depicting the market as a jungle where might is right and where large groups of underprivileged are trampled underfoot, and with the doctrinaire right considering the government as a source of incompetence, inefficiency, and corruption constituting an obstacle to the development of the economy. Both the government and the market are integral components of the economic process. The prospect of anarchy, arbitrary rule, an inequitable income distribution, an inadequate social and physical infrastructure which would result from the government's withdrawal must surely fail to entice any but a very few. On the other hand, experience with centrally controlled systems shows that, without the compass of the price mechanism, it is extremely hard to keep the economy on course and to initiate adjustment to changed circumstances.

It would, therefore, benefit the discussion if the participants are heedful both of the failures of the market mechanism and of the limitations of government action and if, in each individual instance, they attempt to weigh the pros and cons of either option. This will lead to the conclusion that the government should withdraw, in full or in part, from certain sectors or should reduce its influence in these sectors (for the Netherlands a case in point might be housing), but that it should take a more active stance in others (the environment, technology). This changing role of the government, which need not, by definition, be a diminished role, reflects shifts in societal priorities and changing external circumstances and, in some cases, is the result of earlier, undue, government involvement in certain sectors.

Considering the foregoing, I need hardly argue that I am wholly sympathetic to Stiglitz's plea for weighing the pros and cons of government intervention. It must be realized, however, that in this respect a subjective element is unavoidable. Additionally, the optimum role of the government cannot be determined on economic grounds alone; cultural and institutional aspects also exert an influence. These aspects of a country's (political) culture have as a consequence that, for example, Europeans, who are traditionally accustomed to strong government involvement and who in the preceding century experienced the hardships of the adjustment process attending the industrial revolution, tend to take a view of the role of the government which differs from that held by, for instance, the inhabitants of the US, where the pioneering spirit necessary for building an economy in a new and empty world has left an indelible mark on thinking about the government. Even within Europe, differences in culture and tradition may lead to different views of certain government activities. The French, for example, attach great weight to the government's efforts to give guidance to the production process in their country, whereas, influenced by their experiences in the 1930s and 1940s, the Germans are much more cautious in this respect. Government involvement which is felt to be highly successful in one culture may meet with major objections elsewhere, detracting heavily from its efficacy.

There is yet another reason to avoid thinking in unduly black-and-white terms about the economic role of the government. Government involvement may take so many disparate forms (exerting influence on the market sector by subsidies or taxation versus regulation) that a more or less objective assessment of the extent of, and the changes in, such involvement is not nearly possible. Hence, the debate should center not so much on the *extent* of government intervention as on its *form* and its *efficacy*. It might be noted in passing, however, that diminishing the extent could presumably help to enhance efficacy.

In this article, I shall attempt, on the basis of the Dutch situation and Dutch experience of the past decades, to formulate a view of the role of the government. This will not only permit Stiglitz's arguments to be considered from the viewpoint of conditions prevailing in the Netherlands, it may also provide a contribution to the reviving debate, in our country as elsewhere, about whether economic conditions in the 1990s could permit a reassessment of the government's role.

THE GOVERNMENT AS AN ORGANIZATION

The Government's Powers of Compulsion

I concur with Stiglitz when he enumerates universal membership and powers of compulsion as essential characteristics of the State as an organization. Acting in the public interest, the government has power to impose compulsory obligations on its citizens. Within this framework, it may regulate the organization of certain activities of its citizens, prohibit other activities, demand compulsory participation, and impose taxes. Citizens have no choice whether or not to obey. Other organizations which are concerned with promoting public or sectoral interests may also impose certain obligations on their members. However, in cases where a member's interest is incompatible with the sectoral interest, where the costs and benefits of membership are ill-balanced, where a member disagrees with decisions, or where he rejects the organization's leadership, he always has the option to leave the organization.[1] Citizens of a State do not have this option, unless they emigrate.

Limits to the Government's Freedom to Act

I also share Stiglitz's view that certain public goods and services would not be made available on a purely voluntary basis while, on the other hand, the compulsory nature entails certain properties which strongly influence the functioning of the government. At the same time, the characteristics mentioned by Stiglitz also embody the inherent limits to government action. Overemphasizing the government's power to impose ineluctable obligations on its citizens has a danger in that it implies an unduly holistic concept of government and overestimates the government's scope for action. At its most extreme, it would mean that the government is a despot – benevolent or otherwise – who is able and willing to pursue certain aims in a brutal fashion. Although in countries with a one-party system this form of government may be closely approximated, it is not, fortunately, universal. In the more democratic countries, the powers of the government are not unlimited.

More so than Stiglitz, I would stress that the limits are mostly of an institutional nature, even if such aspects as the required application of resources to enforce compliance will definitely play a role in shaping government intervention. In a democracy the government's powers and the manner in which they may be exercised are often attended by the necessary safeguards for the protection of the interests of individuals or minorities. These safeguards may be embodied in statute or may be an integral part of a country's political culture. A case in point is the statutory requirement that certain decisions call for a qualified majority or even unanimous consent. Furthermore, the necessity of allowing for the wishes of other parties in a coalition government, potential parties to a future coalition government, and the electorate limit the government's scope for action. I would even take this one step further. Even if government action were to remain within the limits set out above, that would not be enough for such action to be justified in terms of *substance*, since a truly democratic society – though not formally operating a system of weighted votes – should also reflect minority views.

Breach of Contract

In line with the foregoing, I must object – most definitely if I take the Dutch situation as my perspective – to the categorical assertion that the government is at all times able to go back on earlier obligations and commitments. In this context, it is useful to distinguish between the government's commitments which have been laid down in ordinary contracts and its other commitments embodied in statute or in political pronouncements. Ordinary contracts concluded with individual citizens or enterprises are governed by civil law, so that breach of contract exposes the government to the same sanctions as those which apply to individuals. The legal system and the political culture warrant the government's performance of such obligations and ensure that no revenge will be sought by imposing specific taxes which affect only the citizens or enterprises involved. The situation is different where the second category of commitments is concerned. In a *formal* sense, the government (which I take to be, in this context, the executive legitimized by the legislature) has an ultimate, overruling instrument at its disposal: legislation. In terms of *substance*, however, the government's opportunities for effecting drastic changes in certain statutory arrangements at short notice are severely limited by the political culture. To give an example (leaving aside whether anyone would even contemplate such action): it is inconceivable that sharply rising costs entailed by an aging population would prompt a decision to terminate, all of a sudden, old-age state pensions without any attendant measure to offset its effects. A good example here is afforded by the abolition, early in 1988, of Dutch general premia to stimulate investment. The sudden termination of the arrangement – a highly exceptional move – was attended by practically full compensation in the form of a reduction in both the corporation tax rate and employers' contributions to social insurance. Consequently, in terms of substance, the government's scope for action is severely limited under normal conditions and often allows merely partial adjustment of existing arrangements. In the 1970s the then Dutch socialist Prime Minister, Den Uyl, aptly referred to this as "the narrow margins of policy."

This situation is at the root of the major problems which politicians encounter when attempting to cut public expenditure. Among the public, their electorate, there is a perception of vested rights, even though, in a strictly formal sense, these do not exist. This perception ensues not from stupidity but from confidence inspired by the government. The operational conclusion to be drawn is that the government should proceed most cautiously – at any rate much more cautiously than at present – before undertaking any commitment to intervene (whether such intervention concerns tenant-related rent subsidies, income tax relief for interest paid, or subsidies to enterprises). If commitments, once made, have to be reversed, the public easily gains the impression of "perfidious" government; after all, though it is formally entitled to take such action, the government then fails to proceed with the care which is required in society in dealings with others. An interesting example is provided by the issue of income tax relief for mortgage interest payments. Relying on this relief, citizens undertake burdensome financial obligations for a period of 30 years. Quite apart from the merits of the arrangement itself, canceling this tax relief by amending legislation would grossly violate the confidence created in the past. Hence, any such action would have to be underlaid by very forceful arguments; even so, it would appear questionable whether cancelation would be justifiable for "existing cases."

Limits to Power in Specific Areas

The government's scope for action is limited not only by the need to protect individuals and minority groups but, in some cases, also by special statutory arrangements designed to prevent government action from harming certain aspects of the public interest. A case in point is the organization of monetary policy. In the Netherlands, the legislature has opted for a central bank which is highly independent of the government. This naturally gives rise to the question whether this might lead to an uncontrolled position of power (a state within the State). In the Netherlands this dilemma has been solved by investing the Minister of Finance with the power – to be used only as a measure of last resort and, hence, subject to very strict conditions – to give the bank's governing board directions for the coordination of the bank's monetary policy and the budgetary policy pursued by the government (a power which, incidentally, has never yet been used). In the Federal Republic of Germany, the Bundesbank enjoys an even higher degree of independence as it is not subject to any instructions from the government. However, the *Bundesbankgesetz* provides that "the Federal Bank shall, without prejudice to the fulfilment of its functions, support the general economic policies of the Federal Government." The reason for this arrangement was the fear that politicians might be tempted to subordinate monetary policy to other policy objectives. It was the legislature itself which – with past experience (such as the prewar hyperinflation in Germany) in mind – chose to limit the government's as well as its own scope for action in the monetary field. However, by amending legislation, it may, of course, remove this self-restraint.

MARKET FAILURE AND GOVERNMENT INTERVENTION

With regard to government intervention in the event of market failure, Stiglitz's paper refers to three essential, interrelated problems – also reflected in Dutch government policy – viz: when to intervene; why intervene; how to intervene. I would add a fourth aspect: how to delimit tasks.

The solutions to these problems are not universal and often differ from one country to the next. However, the efficacy of government intervention depends to a considerable extent on the way in which these questions are answered. Consequently, reconsideration of these key decisions offers a powerful tool for enhancing government efficacy; for this reason, these key problems are briefly discussed below.

The Need for Government Intervention

Basically, government intervention ensues from market failure. In this connection, Stiglitz rightly stresses that the problem is not confined to identifying situations of absolute market failure but that the real issue is to decide when market imperfections are such as to warrant intervention. After all, markets are seldom perfect. This complicates the problem considerably and, moreover, leaves room for different views. A definitive answer is possible only if the drawbacks of market failure and those of government intervention can be quantified and compared by some objective method. The difficulties of an adequate trade-off between advantages and disadvantages are illustrated by the ongoing debate, also mentioned by Stiglitz, about the deregulation of financial markets and the supervision of financial institutions, a discussion which naturally plays a dominant role in my job as a central banker. Whereas in past years criticism of regulation, which was considered to have paralyzing and obstructive effects, was predominant, a number of recent financial scandals have prompted a somewhat less negative attitude towards supervision and market regulation.

Conflicting Aims of Government Intervention

Following Musgrave, government intervention may be considered to have as its ultimate aims to improve resource allocation, to encourage stabilization, and to achieve an equitable distribution of income. After World War II, and particularly in the 1970s, the Dutch Government placed major emphasis on the aspects of income distribution, a factor which has had a material influence on the level and the composition of public expenditure. Income transfers to the personal sector constitute far and away the largest component of total public expenditure. The intervention in resource allocation in the areas of health care and housing is in large measure due to this situation.

Sometimes, sharp conflicts may arise between different aims. Measures in the area of income distribution, for instance, have an effect on the operation of the labor market and may thus influence unemployment (the key variable in stabilization policy). In the heavily Keynesian-oriented policies in the Netherlands of the 1970s, this aspect remained underexposed. At the time, the level of unemployment was attributed mainly to underconsumption. In this view, increases in minimum social security benefits and in the related minimum wage level would lead to increased consumption and, hence, to a decrease in unemployment. When, in the 1980s, unemployment increased sharply among the lower-skilled, whose earnings are often at the minimum wage level, more attention was gradually given to the negative effects of a relatively high "floor" in the labor market and of a high degree of leveling of incomes. Ever since, this dilemma has been a central theme in Dutch politics.

Another dilemma may ensue from stabilization policy. A policy of stimulating consumption by increasing public expenditure may thwart the normal process of weighing the pros and cons of the provision of public goods and services. The Dutch situation in the 1970s provides an apt illustration. With a view to stimulating employment, in particular, the Dutch central government decided on considerable outlays in that period on such projects as community centers and municipal swimming pools, which would never have been undertaken by local authorities under normal circumstances; the exploitation costs can sometimes form a heavy burden. At a lower level, too, aims may conflict. It is my impression that the US financial sector is rather averse to (state) supervision, arguing that it may materially affect financial allocation. Unhampered allocation may conflict with another aim, the protection of small depositors. The solution chosen for the savings banks – a low level of supervision and high deposit insurance – has, however, seriously disturbed allocation. It has provided insufficient incentives for a restoration of healthy balance sheet positions after the sharp increase in the general loan loss risk, and has led to a strong preference for high-yield but at the same time high-risk investments.

The Form of Intervention

As demonstrated by Stiglitz, the form of intervention in certain situations may differ substantially from one case to the next. Moreover, some countries would appear to exhibit a bias for certain forms of government intervention. Stiglitz notes that in the US regulation is preferred to action in the areas of taxation or expenditure, whereas, in my opinion, the reverse would sometimes appear to be the case in the Netherlands. At present, lengthy discussions are in progress in the Netherlands about the manner in which environmental problems (such as acid rain) should be tackled in the years ahead. In these discussions, two views are being advanced. Adherents of the first view tend to stress the need for direct measures for combating pollution in the form of general levies and subsidies as well as outlays by the government itself. This view is notably underlaid by the fear that, if the costs of pollution control were to be reflected in selling prices, the country's international competitive position would be unduly depressed. This view, which is the more or less traditional one in the Netherlands, has gradually come to carry less weight as a consequence of the vast budgetary problems with which the Dutch Government has had to cope in the past decade. Adherents of the other view are strongly in favor of regulation, national or international. In this way the costs of environmental protection regulation, such as limits for the emission of harmful wastes, would be reflected in the cost of production, thus ensuring the most efficient allocation of resources possible and doing more justice to the principle that the polluter should foot the bill. Taxes and subsidies, it is argued, have all sorts of side-effects within but also outside of the sectors concerned, such as tendencies to shift the burden of taxation by means of general wage claims, which may have strong adverse effects on the economy in general.

Delimitation of Tasks

Even in cases where government intervention as such is not questioned because the market, as in the case of pure public goods and services, fails to provide goods and services for which there is an evident need, differences of opinion may arise about the quantity to be provided and about the delimitation of tasks. The quantitative aspect will be discussed later. The problem of delimitation centers on the question whether scope ought to be left for private sector initiative. Only rarely will the good or service concerned have solely public aspects. In the Netherlands, for instance, the increase in crime has led to a mushrooming private security industry. Recently, the government took up this issue by pondering whether a limitation of tasks might help to make funds available for use elsewhere within the police force so as to enhance the effectiveness of the fight against crime. In this context, the Minister of Justice held that it was up to the enterprises themselves to ensure the security of their premises, whether or not through joint guard services.

Other areas of government activity, too, such as the administration of justice and education, offer scope for private sector involvement. In the case of the administration of justice, it would be conceivable that contracts might be concluded between industrial organizations and consumer organizations about the institution of committees of arbitration. In the area of education, it is being reviewed whether the extension of student loans might be transferred from the government to the commercial banks.[2] Moreover, many post-doctoral courses are being offered which are financed not from public funds but by the participants themselves and from corporate financial support. Americans will not find any of this very spectacular, but for the Dutch this is very novel indeed.

PUBLIC FAILURE

Lack of Criteria for Action

The government's weaknesses as distinguished by Stiglitz are also evident in the Netherlands. Let me stress first of all that in cases of market failure the government, too, has few clues for determining the optimum level of public provision of goods and services. Where public goods and services are concerned, the criterion that the provision of the goods and services must be increased until marginal costs and marginal societal benefits balance carries little weight, since it is not possible to measure the benefits. Even the costs are difficult to ascertain in the public sector, as the administrative organization is not often suited to providing such information. Like Stiglitz, I hold that improvements in this area are definitely required. Thus far, attempts to strengthen the process of microeconomic evaluation by the central government through the reintroduction of the system whereby current expenditure must be financed from current revenues and only capital expenditure may be financed by borrowing have been unsuccessful in the Netherlands. In other countries, too, microeconomic considerations do not play more than a very minor role in budgetary policies and budget control.

Another variation on this theme is the question whether in cases where the market operates in a basically satisfactory manner, the government might do better. I doubt whether this is likely. Beyond the area of public goods and services, insight into future developments is not such that government intervention will produce better results than market forces. In the 1970s the Dutch Government attempted to prevent destruction of capital by providing massive support to enterprises in financial difficulties; the underlying view was that the problems were caused merely by a temporary fall in demand. This perception was belied by later developments, and, ultimately, major restructuring efforts, attended by large-scale redundancies, proved unavoidable. I need not argue that I am not among the advocates of indicative planning. Not only because, for whatever reasons, the government lacks the ability to respond flexibly to market changes but also because it often lacks the intuitive affinity with the market which is necessary to estimate future trends and to identify favorable growth opportunities. This does not, however, alter the fact that in the area of market order the government definitely has a role to play.

Pressure Groups and the Influence of the Civil Service

The lack of objective standards for the determination of the optimum volume of public goods and services, the lack of transparency of the decision-making process, and the lack of insight into the effects of revenue and expenditure lead to a situation where active lobbying may be successful. In the public-choice literature, this phenomenon is extensively analyzed by such authors as Buchanan, Downs, Tullock, and Olson. As in other countries, pressure groups are part of the political folklore in the Netherlands, even if they would appear to have lost some of their influence in the 1980s as a result of the limited financial scope of the government. The interests of the civil service, too, play a considerable role in decision making and policy implementation; this will be discussed in some detail later in the context of decentralization and privatization. Unexposed to competition, the civil service tends to exert constant pressure to maintain or, preferably, to increase employment. Reallocation of resources, too, is frustrated from within the civil service, but the latter problem is evident in the business sector as well.

Safeguards against Abuse of Power

The other government weaknesses, as advanced by Stiglitz, regarding the choice of leadership, the constraints imposed on the flexibility of the civil service by the incorporation of safeguards against favoritism in appointments, pay matters, and dismissal, are, in a sense, present in the Netherlands as well, although, in my view, their effects are modest.

In the Netherlands, the electoral system is concerned with parties rather than persons; ministers are also recruited from those outside the direct realm of politics because of their expertise and management skills rather than their political qualifications.

Safeguards in the areas of appointment, pay, and dismissal as well as procedures designed to prevent corruption and abuses of power are admittedly present, but it might be wondered whether, except for dismissal procedures, they differ greatly from those in operation in large enterprises. It is true, however, that the pay system is not tailored to provide financial incentives for good performance, but this is also due to a lack of insight into performance. In some segments of industry, and notably in the services sector and in the case of administrative jobs, the link between performance and pay may, incidentally, also be very weak. The Dutch Government is aware of this problem and is seeking to curb the system of automatic wage increases for civil servants and to create more scope for financial incentives in the case of good performance. Furthermore, considering the strongly Calvinistic streak in Dutch culture, tolerating corruption, favoritism, etc. would involve tremendous electoral risks.

IMPROVING GOVERNMENT EFFICACY AND EFFICIENCY

To counter the potential shortcomings in the public sector, Stiglitz recommends enhancing the role of competition within this sector. In this respect, possibilities for improvement include sharing the production of public goods and services with the private sector, and decentralization.

Since the early 1980s, the need for checking the strong growth of the public sector has meant that in the Netherlands much attention has been focused on these areas, in line with international trends. Below, a brief discussion is given of the Dutch experience to date.

Privatization

Privatization was boosted by studies which showed that, in some cases, private sector enterprises operated 20 to 50 percent more efficiently than comparable public enterprises. However, by contrast with the UK and, recently, France, where privatization consists in the sale of state enterprises engaged in steel-making, aircraft construction, oil exploration, banking, etc., privatization in the Netherlands centers on tasks actually performed by the government itself. This concerns operations relating to natural monopolies (e.g. postal and telecommunications services) and services to the business sector (pilotage, inspection of weights and measures) on the one hand, and segments of government agencies which have independent counterparts in the business sector (accountancy services, printing works, computer centers, cleaning services, refuse-disposal services, and park maintenance services) on the other. It is true that the Dutch Government is also selling public enterprises which operate in the market as well as participations in enterprises; however, as socialization has never gained widespread acceptance in the Netherlands and as the government has never sought to capture key positions in (heavy) industry or banking through nationalization, the extent of such privatization is limited. Recently, the government sold part of its 100 percent holding in DSM (Dutch State Mines) on the stock exchange. (DSM was originally engaged in coal exploitation and processing but is now a major producer of chemicals.) Additionally, minority holdings in KLM (Royal Dutch Airlines), Fokker (aircraft), Nederlandsche Middenstandsbank, and some other enterprises have been sold.

One of the principal problems involved in the privatization efforts in the Netherlands is the legal status of civil servants. Privatization causes employees to lose their status as civil servants, facing them with financial disadvantages as regards pension and social security benefits. Furthermore, wage rates under private sector labor agreements may be lower. Hence, the civil servants' unions often fiercely oppose privatization. For higher-level staff, this is frequently different, since pay levels for such staff are mostly higher in the private sector. Another problem is the obligation to charge value-added tax. As government agencies are exempt from this obligation, privatization causes production cost, other conditions remaining equal, to increase by as much as about 20 percent. Consequently, substantial efficiency gains are necessary if privatization of (parts) of production is to be at all attractive for the government agency in question.

Privatization may also give rise to specific problems if the supply side and/or the demand side is marked by near or full monopoly or monopsony respectively. In the latter case, the government or a comparable agency is the sole buyer. In my work as a central banker, I have first-hand experience of such situations in the area of banknotes and coins, where, for reasons pertaining to security and economies of scale, production is often centralized. Here, privatization is admittedly possible in a formal sense, yet difficult to attain in actual practice. In this context, I am referring not to historical and emotional considerations which argue against privatization but to the dominant influence of the single buyer (the State or the central bank) on the single producer. It is very hard in such cases to resist cost-plus contracts, which remove any incentive to improve efficiency. For such enterprises, the real issue is not their formal status but the conditions under which they operate. It is, for instance, most helpful if the State or the central bank is prepared to keep the pressure on by occasionally ordering banknotes or coins from an enterprise abroad.

Although, meanwhile, more than 113,000 of the total of 561,000 central government jobs have been privatized, this should not be viewed as earthshaking. In most cases, the privatization concerned the granting of independent status to public enterprises (postal and telecommunications services). However, all shares in these independent enterprises continue to be held by the government. Hiving-off of activities in the sense that the government contracts out the work without an obligation to favor any privatized government agencies accounts for a mere 8,000 of the total of 113,000 privatized jobs. If a publicly owned enterprise is granted independent status, government influence on production is not eliminated, though it does become more indirect, creating an arm's length relationship between government and enterprise. This may bring about a change in corporate culture towards more business-like attitudes, benefiting efficacy and efficiency. Consequently, the granting of independent status is to be viewed as an intermediate stage in privatization.

Territorial Decentralization[3]

In 1980 the Dutch Government embarked upon decentralization, advancing the following as the advantages it offered:

1. better opportunities for tailoring output to consumer needs;
2. increased accessibility for, and more democratic influence by, citizens;
3. greater freedom and variation for local authorities;
4. increased efficacy and efficiency;
5. better control of public expenditure.

The policy sought to replace part of the so-called specific grants (central government grants to local authorities subject to strict spending conditions) by general grants, disbursed on the basis of general apportionment criteria, such as number of inhabitants, degree of urbanization, etc. In the case of general grants, the local authorities may spend the funds at their discretion. Specific grants have a drawback in that they involve considerable bureaucracy at both the central and the local levels and that, despite extensive reporting obligations, those who decide on the application of the funds have little insight into the efficacy and efficiency with which the funds are actually spent. This "expense account" system fails to provide the spending authorities with any incentives to limit costs.

Surprisingly, opposition to decentralization is evident not only at central government level but at the local level as well. For the central government level, this was to be expected since decentralization undermines the position of the civil service. The opposition at the local level ensues from problems of distribution and from fear of hidden expenditure cuts. Since the original arrangements were designed to suit specific conditions and situations, such as the number of historic buildings in a certain area, those local authorities which now receive considerable amounts might receive less if the arrangements were to be changed to provide for general rather than specific grants. Hence, for these local authorities the advantages of increased policy freedom do not balance the financial disadvantages. Attempts to phase in systems of general grants to replace specific grants inevitably call forth varying choruses of protest, with fears that this will provide the central government with a handle to shift expenditure cuts to the local authorities as the constant background theme. It cannot, incidentally, be denied that some of the central government's past actions have fueled this distrust. When asked for proposals to implement decentralization, the local authorities themselves mainly suggest cutting red tape rather than converting specific grants into general ones.

Stiglitz expects that decentralization will lead to competition between local authorities and that citizens will take up residence where they find the most attractive mix of public goods and services provided and local taxes levied. This is definitely not inconceivable. Competition between local communities is already evident in their policies to stimulate establishment of enterprises, with land prices, site infrastructure, and other conditions of establishment being used as incentives. This competition has already caused the system of land leasehold to be discarded to a major extent, considering the profound lack of confidence which both enterprises and citizens evince towards the authorities where the future movements in leasehold charges are concerned.

AN OUTLINE OF THE ROLE OF THE DUTCH GOVERNMENT IN THE 1990S

The key question which we shall have to answer in the years ahead is not *whether* the government should play a role – to my mind, that is beyond question – but *how* it should perform this role and how it should seek to improve its efficacy and efficiency.

The policy to be pursued in the coming years is in large measure governed by existing legislation and the consequent obligations as well as by the government's present commitments. In the longer run these may, of course, be changed but, as noted before, the available margins are often narrow. In this respect, the image of a supertanker springs to mind, not only with regard to the volume of public expenditure but also with regard to the government's opportunities to adjust course. In addition, opposition from the civil service, conflicts of interest between government agencies, and influence exerted by pressure groups make change a laborious process. The limited ability to check processes, once they have been set in motion, calls for restraint, even in periods offering more financial scope, in initiating new programs, especially if the financial effects in later years are not clear.

In this context, I should like to make a plea for a system of budgeting which encourages policy makers to take a longer view. Instead of a system which concentrates solely on the financial scope in the year ahead and on the claims made on that scope, all of which are heavily dependent on the prevailing economic conditions, I would prefer medium-term agreements on the *permissible* development of expenditure. Confronting this medium-term financial framework with the medium-term expenditure estimates (extrapolations of existing and planned policies) would serve to identify bottlenecks at an early stage and would thus permit appropriate measures to be taken in good time. It would help to prevent ad hoc decision making from year to year, with expenditure policy being heavily dominated by budget variances in respect of revenues, a situation which easily leads to stop-go policies.

Like any other organization, the government cannot escape the need for adjustment to changed circumstances. For the government, too, flexibility is essential; the opportunities for resource reallocation must be a subject of permanent review. Resource reallocation demands an insight not only into priorities but also into posteriorities. A lower priority need not, incidentally, always mean that the task concerned must be hived off completely. Within the present range of government activities, too, funds may be released by considering other methods of government intervention or redefining tasks and allowing room for private sector initiatives. Careful and in-depth screening of certain activities by means of parliamentary enquiries has revealed a number of government failures in the Netherlands and has given rise to questions as to the efficacy of certain measures. As a result, a number of tasks have been hived off or have been drastically streamlined. This goes to show that periodic screening of certain activities, if properly embedded in the political framework, may contribute to reallocation of resources.

The need for resource reallocation in the years ahead is enhanced by the fact that the environmental policy and the increasing costs entailed by the ever-larger percentage of old-age pensioners in the population will require considerable amounts of additional funds. Training of the long-term unemployed and other programs for the re-employment of this category demand extra efforts. The possibility of financing these programs from the scope afforded by economic growth are only limited as the central government's financial deficit, in terms of national income, must be reduced in the years ahead by 2 to 3 percentage points so as to check the growth of national debt in relative terms. Increases in taxation and social insurance contributions are not a viable option either. For an improvement in the Dutch competitive position, continued wage restraint is essential. Hence, emphasis should be placed on cuts in taxes and social insurance contributions, since they are conducive to wage restraint. However, to create room for such cuts, it is all the more necessary to release funds by reallocation of resources and by enhancing the government's efficiency. This calls for profound reflection on the government's role in the economy.

From the foregoing, it will be clear that, in my view, the ideal extent of government influence and of government intervention cannot be ascertained on the basis of immutable principles. Rather, resort must be had to processes of trial and error, of learning from experience, and of consequent adjustment of policies in order to optimize the government's role in the economy.

NOTES

1 There are, incidentally, certain forms of cooperative societies in Dutch agriculture, where resigning one's membership is difficult, if not impossible. It is worthy of note that these societies, which often run factories for the processing of agricultural raw materials, were set up on a voluntary basis by private persons to prevent farmers from being exploited by private purchasers of agricultural produce and, hence, clearly served a general interest. Thus, in some cases the distinction between compulsory and voluntary membership may merely be one of degree.
2 In this respect, the situation in the Netherlands differs from that in the US, where it is proposed that the government should grant such loans itself and/or collect the repayments of these loans by the tax system (see Stiglitz).
3 Functional decentralization, towards which initiatives have been taken in the Netherlands as well, will not be discussed in this contribution.

Comments 6

Sir Ian MacGregor

Professor Stiglitz's paper examines and identifies many of the functions of government and brings them into perspective with a degree of objectivity. We recognize that in the more sophisticated societies such as the US, Europe, and Japan the activities of government have increased continuously and enormously. When we compare the role of government today with what it was even just 50 years ago, it is remarkable the extent to which government impact on all aspects of our lives has grown and become increasingly pervasive. There have been periods, especially in the last two decades, when concern about the extent of government encroachment in our everyday affairs has become an important political issue – when, for example, President Carter ran his campaign in the late 1970s in part on the basis that he would go to Washington to try to reduce the government impact on the lives of the citizens. He wasn't totally successful in this campaign, although he did deregulate the airlines with a very dramatic impact (certainly at first) on the cost of flying and the availability of flying services in the US. However, the pervasiveness of government still concerns many people, especially those who are engaged in any activities of commerce, industry, and business.

There is, of course, the public dichotomy on this issue, as is pointed out by Professor Stiglitz. We all would seek to conduct our affairs with a minimum of interference from others, especially from government, but that doesn't reduce the public urge to press government authority to impose some rule to correct some perceived (or imagined) injustice. We all understand the wide differences between government, with its ability to impose its will, and any other form of cooperative endeavor, in which we have the choice either of participating or, as Professor Stiglitz puts it, exiting, leaving and opting out. But government has the power of compulsion which leaves many people with an underlying feeling of unease and concern. In my mind, it may be because, when we look back over recent decades, there have developed some rather unattractive situations where government took its ability to compel very seriously. The outstanding example of the century, of course, is Germany of the 1930s. But it is only one of many in this century. In another way the emergence of the socialist republics of the Eastern Bloc has depended very heavily on government's ability to compel and to impose ideology, ideas, and will upon the population at large.

We are now beginning to see that some of these systems do not seem to be able to perform or improve conditions to the extent that they attract the unqualified support of those who are governed. In all of these situations, it is difficult to see where the line between support for and compulsion by government is established. One assumes that at one stage, in the early days of the Eastern European socialist governments, there was a substantial degree of support, on the grounds that these were new ideas in government and could, perhaps, produce benefits of a widespread nature for people who, up to that time, had seen very little benefit from the overall economic capability of the society in which they lived. Likewise in Germany in the late 1920s and early 1930s, there was no question but that a very large number of people looked to the emerging Third Reich as a new idea which was different and offered better opportunities than the bleak decade of the 1920s. The problems of reparations and the burdens that these imposed on society had produced for the average German looking into the future a very unhappy and unapparently unrelieved situation of gloom. The early promise of a different Germany with hope and power and self-respect and a command of the situation appealed to many Germans. Later that system of government moved into a period where compulsion in a very high degree was essential in order to sustain the authority of the government.

But what is it that concerns us about government? Leo Tolstoy identified the yearning for freedom as one of the strongest of human instincts. What he said was, "All men's instincts, all their impulses in life, are only efforts to increase their freedom – wealth and poverty, health and disease, culture and ignorance, labor and leisure, repletion and hunger, virtue and vice, are only terms for greater or lesser degrees of freedom." In each situation, good or bad health, wealth or poverty, leisure or labor were seen as opposite poles of freedom or restriction for the individual. Poor health certainly restricts. Poverty restricts. Tolstoy believed it was a natural instinct for the human race to try to achieve freedom by enjoying the better of each of these alternatives. Obviously, we all, I think, agree that these are factors which make a human existence infinitely more pleasant and bearable. But total freedom of action has to be qualified in a modern society. I think we have all accepted that we have to live within certain rules and regulations in order to ensure that the exercise of our freedom of action does not disadvantage others. One of the problems facing modern society is to differentiate between the responsibilities of freedom and the license which some individuals seem to feel is necessary perhaps to bolster their egos. If people are free in their exercise of all of their assumed rights in society, there can be a dichotomy with the interests of others, as we observe in such manifestations as football hooliganism. I can cite numerous examples where people exercise what they perceive to be their inalienable right to freedom of action and thus cause enormous discomfort, concern, and inconvenience to their fellow citizens.

The emergence of a political following for the concern about the growth of government and its increasing intervention in the regulation and lives of individuals did result in movements in many of our democratic countries towards a re-examination of the role of government. In some instances there was recognition that government had overreached itself both in regulation and in other functions, including production. The movement towards less government intervention took different forms in different countries. In the US, the ambition was to reduce regulation and deregulate where possible, and I have cited one example – the airline industry. In the UK, government stake in the economy had gone far beyond the regulatory phase. As Britain moved towards socialism after World War II, the socialists' doctrine of the nationalization of the instruments of production became an extremely important plank in the platform of the socialist governments that succeeded one another. Even in the UK in the 1970s there was a considerable body of public opinion which had concluded that the government was probably less successful than private concerns in the production phase of the economy. Thus, the Thatcher government emerged in 1979 with considerable political support from the idea that government's intervention should be reduced and that the trend towards the nationalization of industrial production should be reversed.

This came at the end of a decade when many of the industries which were nationalized immediately after the war, or which in some cases had seesawed back and forth between the nationalized sector and the private sector, were clearly seen to be far less successful than they should have been. They also seemed to be less responsive to the public's needs in the marketplace. For example, the nationalized British car industry enjoyed a very poor reputation with car buyers and saw a dramatic decline in its share of the market during the late 1970s. In the same way the steel industry, which went through the on-again, off-again nationalization cycle, entered the decade of the 1970s totally nationalized. Again, it had generated a reputation for being less responsive to its customers' needs. Finally, at the end of the 1970s, a long work stoppage forced many customers loyal to the steel industry to look abroad at a time which coincided with the early coalescing of the European economy. As Britain was a newcomer to the community in the late 1970s, there had not been a great development of UK community trade. All at once steel users in the UK found that European supplies were available and many times could serve them better – and even more cheaply – than the production of the nationalized industry at home. Politically, the Thatcher administration seized on the public's perception of the ineffectiveness of nationalized industry to weld together a political program, which envisaged a combination of deregulation and denationalization and wide share ownership in the former government-owned enterprises.

Professor Stiglitz has carefully analyzed the pros and cons of nationalized industrial activity. As he brings out, the objectives of these industries are not always clear-cut. They have a number of sometimes contradictory objectives imposed on them by the political pressures to which they are infinitely more subject than private enterprise would be. The record shows that the Thatcher approach to converting these industries back to the private sector has been quite successful, not only in relieving the government of substantial loss-making activities, with their debilitating effect upon the national budget, but also in producing the opportunities for better service for the users of those services. This is clearly seen in the case of British Airways. One of the most dramatic examples was the privatization of the national freight hauling system, in which the major portion of the truck industry was turned back to private owners. Many of the new owners were employees in the business. In fact, it can be seen as one of the first and probably one of the more successful LBO's. Since then other industries have joined in this trend. Now the government is tackling some of the more difficult ones, where normal market forces are distorted by monopoly or quasi-monopoly situations, as in the case of the public electricity and water supplies. Here the future will involve careful design of regulation and efforts to improve the potential for competition within the industries, although these are very difficult goals to accomplish.

What we are really looking at, of course, is the problem which faces governments with regard to the regulation of industry and commerce. It has been a desire on the part of many of the political supporters of the UK Conservative government to see market forces dominate and dictate conditions. It is now emerging that such arrangements are not always possible, and certainly pure competition is very difficult to achieve in the complicated society in which we live. The future of this bold initiative will depend on the success of combining maximum use of market forces with a careful degree of regulation which seeks to avoid the excesses of total regulation. Excessive regulation has occurred in some areas of US industry, such as airlines in the last decade and the electric power supply industry in this decade. The collapse of the nuclear industry in the US is an example of what can happen if the public's perceptions lead to excessive regulatory activity, making it almost impossible for private capital to operate. One assessment of what has happened to the nuclear industry in the US would suggest that over-zealous regulation, coupled as it was with constantly changing standards and public environmental perceptions, has made the construction of plants to produce nuclear electricity by private capital almost impossible. There is great difficulty in establishing, at the time a project is initiated, what conditions it will have to operate under when it is completed some seven, eight, or ten years later. I think if you will examine the collapse of the nuclear power generation program in the US you will find this to be the principal ingredient in its failure.

During the last couple of decades, we have seen the economic world converge. Today we have essentially one capital market which encircles the globe, and no country has achieved any way to insulate itself from the effects of the global flow of capital and money. In the decades ahead, I believe we will see a rather similar development in the political field, moving towards a convergence of political experiences and ideas.

What is emerging in China and now in the USSR is the apparent acceptance that the idea of central planning and control and regulation of every aspect of the economic machine in a given national environment produces poorer results than those emanating from the more rigid and rugged disciplines of the marketplace. The convergence that I see is a movement on the part of the socialists towards a greater decentralization of the planning function and the progressive decentralization of control to make the economy more susceptible to the needs of the consumer as he perceives them rather than as the government perceives them. At the same time the market economies will be moving towards systems of more regulation that are sufficiently responsive to imbalances or distortions which might excessively favor the enterprise which is providing the service or the goods.

An example of this might be seen in the recent history of the nationalized natural gas industry in the UK, which started as a national monopoly. It has now moved into the private sector with a system of regulation which is still not fully worked out, but is addressed to identifying and correcting distortions in the service or pricing policies resulting from its private monopoly. At the same time, some tentative arrangements have been made to enable others to participate in part of the market. A concern that is emerging from this, as with the US telephone industry, is the problem of cross-subsidization. In the US telephone industry case, we are about to see the effects of cross-subsidization being eliminated, and I suspect that many of the users will find the results of the subsequent scramble by providers to share markets not necessarily to their liking. Many are concerned that the rush to provide cost-competitive services may reduce the reliability and dependability to which they have been accustomed and for which many feel they were quite prepared to pay.

In the Western economies, then, it now looks as if the political idea that the government should be a provider of goods and services is in a decline. Professor Stiglitz has outlined many of the reasons why this political trend has received growing acceptance. What happens next, however, is more likely to be a move towards the convergence I referred to, as private sector provision of most of our requirements in goods and services is enlarged and in many instances covers fields in which there are quasi-monopolies. The need for regulation will increasingly require governments to play a new role as the arbiters not only of quality but of service and even of price. We have already seen some of this in the monopoly industries, but it may well be the wave of the future. Thus the free market economies may evolve systems which are in part market dominated but which still require government intervention in regulating systems to avoid unfair exploitation of the free market.

I suspect it was concern about the recognition of this role in the emerging domination of the EEC by big brother Brussels that has been disturbing to some in the UK. The speech made by Mrs Thatcher at Bruges was an expression of her concern about the growing preoccupation in Brussels with regulation of all facets of economic and social life in the EEC. That is why I have used the word "convergence." The West may well be faced with many of the problems that those in the Eastern regulated economies have had to put up with and which they now wish, in their new-found freedom, to see diminished, if not removed.

Comments 7

Jean-Jacques Laffont

Professor Stiglitz has given us a brilliant synthesis of what economic theory can say about the role of the State in the economy. He has touched on too many issues to deal with them in any detail with a few comments.

Two of the major roles of the government are redistribution and regulation and Professor Stiglitz has discussed these separately. There exists indeed a foundation for such a dichotomous treatment, namely the famous Atkinson–Stiglitz theorem, which establishes sufficient (and reasonable) conditions for the irrelevance of indirect taxation in redistributive taxation. As Professor Stiglitz is also a founding father of the economics of information, it might be interesting to show how incomplete information restores a necessary link between the two essential branches of the activity of the State that regulation and redistributive taxation constitute.

For this purpose I will use a simplistic model which could be developed into a more rigorous and general model only at great cost.

Consider an economy with two types of consumer. Type 1 consumers have a utility function $V(q_1) + x_1$, where q_1 is the consumption of commodity 1 produced by the regulated firm and x_1 is the aggregate of other goods, say money. The income distribution of type 1 consumers has mean $\bar{y}_1$. Type 2 consumers have a utility function $S(q_2, q_3) + x_2$ where q_2 is also produced by the regulated firm, q_3 is produced at a price β_3 by a competitive industry with constant marginal cost β_3, and x_2 is money. The income distribution of type 2 consumers has mean $\bar{y}_2$. Incomes are not observable and range for each type of consumer from zero to infinity. Consequently, if the State does not want to run the risk of bankruptcy, "income" taxation is excluded. Moreover, we assume that *individual* consumptions of goods 1, 2, and 3 are not observable so that only linear taxes are possible on these goods.

Suppose next that the State wishes to redistribute income to type 1, an idea that we will formalize by assuming that the weight α of type 1 consumers in the social welfare function is higher than unity. The technology of the regulated firm is described by its cost function

$$C = C(\beta, e, q_1, q_2)$$

where β is a technological parameter in $[\underline{\beta}, \overline{\beta}]$ known only to the firm, the function C is common knowledge, and e is an effort variable which decreases costs and which has a disutility $\psi(e)$ ($\psi' > 0$, $\psi'' > 0$, $\psi''' > 0$) for the firm that is unobservable by the regulator. A regulation mechanism is equivalent to a revelation mechanism $t(\beta)$, $q_1(\beta)$, $q_2(\beta)$, $C(\beta)$ which induces truth-telling by the firm. The firm maximizes with respect to its answer $\tilde{\beta}$:

$$t(\tilde{\beta}) - \psi[E(\beta, C(\tilde{\beta}), q_1(\tilde{\beta}), q_2(\tilde{\beta}))]$$

where E is the inverse function of

$$C = C(\beta, e, q_1, q_2)$$

The first-order incentive compatibility condition is

$$\dot{t}(\beta) + \psi'[E_C \dot{C}(\beta) + E_{q_1} \dot{q}_1(\beta) + E_{q_2} \dot{q}_2(\beta)] = 0$$

We will neglect second-order conditions which can be easily dealt with, at least in some cases.

Let

$$U(\beta) = t(\beta) - \psi[E(\beta, C(\beta), q_1(\beta), q_2(\beta))]$$

It is the rent of asymmetric information extracted by the firm of characteristic β. The incentive compatibility condition can be rewritten

$$\dot{U}(\beta) = -\psi'[e(\beta)] E_\beta \quad (1)$$

As $\dot{U}(\beta)$ is a decreasing function of β the participation constraint of the firm (individual rationality constraint) can be written

$$U(\overline{\beta}) \geq 0 \quad (2)$$

Moreover, the regulator knows that consumers maximize utility under their budget constraints. Therefore if p_1, p_2 are the (consumer) prices of the goods produced by the regulated firm we have

$$V_1(q_1) - p_1 = 0 \quad (3)$$

$$\frac{\partial S(q_2, q_3)}{\partial q_2} - p_2 = 0 \qquad (4)$$

Finally, the regulator has a budget constraint that we write in expectations:

$$\int_{\underline{\beta}}^{\bar{\beta}} [p_1(\beta)q_1(\beta) + p_2(\beta)q_2(\beta)] \, dF(\beta)$$

$$= \int_{\underline{\beta}}^{\bar{\beta}} \{C[\beta, e, q_1(\beta), q_2(\beta)] + U(\beta) + \psi[e(\beta)]\} \, dF(\beta) \qquad (5)$$

where $F(\beta)$ is the cumulative distribution function describing the regulator's expectations about β.

The regulator wishes to maximize expected social welfare under the above constraints, i.e.

$$\max \int_{\underline{\beta}}^{\bar{\beta}} \{\alpha[V(q_1) + \bar{y}_1 - p_1 q_1] + [S(q_2, q_3) + \bar{y}_2 - p_2 q_2 - \beta_3 q_3] + U\} \, dF(\beta)$$

under (1), (2), (3), (4), and (5).

The Hamiltonian of the program is

$$H = \{\alpha[V(q_1) + \bar{y}_1 - p_1 q_1] + [S(q_2, q_3) + \bar{y}_2 - p_2 q_2 - \beta_3 q_3] + U\} f(\beta)$$

$$- \mu(\beta)\psi'(e)E_\beta + \delta[p_1 q_1 + p_2 q_2 - C(\beta, e, q_1, q_2) - U - \psi(e)] f(\beta)$$

From the Pontryagin principle we have

$$\dot{\mu}(\beta) = -\frac{\partial \mu}{\partial U} = -(1 - \delta)f(\beta)$$

Using the transversality condition $\mu(\bar{\beta}) = 0$ we obtain

$$\mu(\beta) = -\int_{\underline{\beta}}^{\beta} (1 - \delta) \, dF(\beta) = (\delta - 1)F(\beta)$$

Maximization with respect to q_1, q_2, p_1, p_2, and e gives

$$\alpha\left(\frac{\partial V}{\partial q_1} - p_1\right)f(\beta) - (\delta - 1)F(\beta)\psi'(e)\frac{\partial E_\beta}{\partial q_1} + \delta(p_1 - Cq_1)f(\beta)$$
$$+ V_1(\beta)f(\beta)V''(q_1) = 0 \qquad (6)$$

$$\left(\frac{\partial S}{\partial q_2} - p_2\right)f(\beta) - (\delta - 1)F(\beta)\psi'(e)\frac{\partial E_\beta}{\partial q_2}$$
$$+ \delta(p_2 - Cq_2)f(\beta) + V_2(\beta)f(\beta)\frac{\partial^2 S}{\partial q_2^2} = 0 \qquad (7)$$

$$-\alpha q_1 f(\beta) + \delta q_1 f(\beta) - V_1(\beta)f(\beta) = 0 \qquad (8)$$

$$-q_2 f(\beta) + \delta q_2 f(\beta) - V_2(\beta)f(\beta) = 0 \qquad (9)$$

$$\psi'(e) = -Ce - \frac{\delta - 1}{\delta}\frac{F(\beta)}{f(\beta)}\psi''(e)$$

The last equation specifies the incentive scheme used to regulate the firm. The derivative $\psi'(e)$ can be interpreted as the coefficient sharing the overruns of the firm (at least under some further convexity restrictions). From (8) and (9)

$$V_1(\beta) = (\delta - \alpha)q_1$$
$$V_2(\beta) = (\delta - 1)q_2$$

From (6) and (7) we obtain the optimal pricing equations:

$$\frac{p_1 - Cq_1}{p_1} = \frac{\delta - \alpha}{\delta}\frac{1}{\eta_1} + \frac{\delta - 1}{\delta}\frac{F(\beta)}{f(\beta)}\frac{\psi'(e)}{p_1}\frac{\partial E_\beta}{\partial q_1}$$

$$\frac{p_2 - Cq_2}{p_2} = \frac{\delta - 1}{\delta}\frac{1}{\eta_2} + \frac{\delta - 1}{\delta}\frac{F(\beta)}{f(\beta)}\frac{\psi'(e)}{p_2}\frac{\partial E_\beta}{\partial q_2}$$

where η_i is the price elasticity of good i.

These pricing formulae equate the Lerner index $L_i = (p_i - Cq_i)/p_i$ to a Ramsey term

$$R_1 = \frac{\delta - \alpha}{\delta} \frac{1}{\eta_1}$$

or

$$R_2 = \frac{\delta - 1}{\delta} \frac{1}{\eta_2}$$

plus an incentive correction

$$I_i = \frac{\delta - 1}{\delta} \frac{F(\beta)}{f(\beta)} \frac{\psi'(e)}{p_i} \frac{\partial E_\beta}{\partial q_i}$$

They generalize the Ramsey equations to deal with incentives. The dichotomy theorem states that if $C = C[\phi(\beta, e), q_1, q_2]$ then the incentive terms vanish. Incentives and pricing can be dealt with separately. In this simple case the pricing equations reduce to

$$\frac{p_1 - Cq_1}{p_1} = \frac{\delta - \alpha}{\delta} \frac{1}{\eta_1}$$

$$\frac{p_2 - Cq_2}{p_2} = \frac{\delta - 1}{\delta} \frac{1}{\eta_2}$$

The price of good 2 exceeds the marginal costs because public funds have a social cost that is higher than unity. Moreover, because the regulator wishes to redistribute income towards type 1 consumers, the price–marginal cost margin is reduced for the good consumed by type 1 consumers.

In this way we obtain justification for Posner's taxation by regulation, i.e. for the use of regulation to realize some redistribution in a world where direct income taxes are not optimal. Any distortion of income taxes away from the optimum may be a foundation for the interaction between regulation and taxation.

Of course the results obtained here are not immune to various criticisms made by Professor Stiglitz either on regulation or on taxation. We have not enquired what the origin was of the social welfare function that we have postulated and we certainly cannot escape the need for constructing a political economy of taxation as well as regulation. In such a theory, which I have started to develop with Jean Jirole, rent-seeking activities and more generally coalitional behavior and collusions between regulators and agents will have to be taken into account.

Also, the fundamental issue of the scope of regulation raised by Professor Stiglitz cannot be escaped even in our simple model. We have postulated that good 3 was sold at marginal cost in a competitive industry. Why not extend regulation to good 3 also? It would certainly be beneficial in our model. Commitment limitations but probably also more difficult phenomena such as unforecastable events as well as direct costs of regulation will be some of the building blocks of a theory of the scope of regulation which remains to be constructed. By taking seriously into account the decentralization of information, Professor Stiglitz has shown that public economics, in the extended (non-American) sense of the word he uses, must be reconsidered to include discussions of incentives and corruption. Competition and decentralization appear to be imperfect ways to police these difficulties.

I believe that Professor Stiglitz's points are highly important not because they are new or deep but because they are made at the right time, i.e. at a time when they are ripe for economic analysis. This is hardly surprising from a man who has been at the frontier of research for the last 20 years.